CW01501256

This is not your ordinary book. I had little interest in titling it as there's nothing to advertise here. It's more of a reaction; a consequence of biting my mind until it bled.

SOMETHING, SOMETHING PUBLISHERS
66-33A, someplace, somewhere, avaricious people.
First published 1995, Sydney, Australia, after having my first thought.
Copyright © no one. Do whatever the hell you want with this book.
Author - Travis Jake Woods
Me, I, yes, it's mine, mine! Muahaha!

CONTENTS

Greetings, I appear before you through symbols though my presence is authentic. Like yourself, I'm alive. I'm what seems to be a temporary materialised wave of the great energy behind this cosmic endeavour, vibrating and hallucinating a dream-like world. I write that while scrunching my face because it's hard to make sense of myself, let alone anything.

If you're reading this, whatever, wherever, whenever you are, I hope this experience isn't too painful for you. Sometimes I find it challenging and want out of here; a part of me doesn't correlate well with my physicality. It's repeatedly banging against my three-dimensional conditions. Known as the mind, it hosts a matrix from which ego persists. For example, I write this while my remarkable physical self motions many bizarre activities such as cellular operations and neurological transmissions. The predicament is conflicting. I dream of flying, but I can't. I imagine dancing with 'her,' yet feel no one. I can, however, alter the primary channel of consciousness to bodily experience, usually through meditative practices for relief, but I'm fascinated by attempting to intellectualise my entirety, so I often hang out in the domain of mind to philosophise through ego. There's also soul or spirit, but no words are best to explain that part of my being.

I share this world with other humans too - creatures biologically formed like myself. I presume you're one, but who knows how far or where these words will travel and what can translate them.
In my time, civilisation, society, culture - the general feeling is a lack of connection. Not just between what I mentioned earlier of mind and body, but self and other, time and moment, space and nature. We have these funny, trivial concepts such as race and nationality, and people take them so seriously. They even become violent, but I believe they're afraid. Everyone's on edge, though that's understandable when before us is a fall.

See, I'm of a mortal plane; everything here dies. Even celestial bodies such as my home star will inevitably end. As much as death is necessary for life, it contradicts us, almost jokingly. I find it to be that as well, comical, and being in on the joke is a lot better than having it go right over your head.

So I choose to see myself as a gag, surprise; otherwise, the pain is too excruciating. Hence, I hope I can smile as I die, after the fear, the moment I let go of this realm. I may have entered this realm screaming, but I'm heading out laughing.

I'm also trying my best to have as many days as I can where I do nothing but soak in the sunlight, dance wildly, write poetry, watch birds fly and embrace a simple life. Because when I get to the bottom of what feels most meaningful, it's the environment in which nothing is happening but the happening. There's nothing significant going on relative to productivity or progression; it's just my fellow kind jumping around to music and laughing with each other. However, it doesn't always go this way. There are plenty of moments where I feel hurt, though when this occurs, I try to remember it's still a moment of feeling, an indication I'm alive, here, undergoing the negative so I can know ecstasy.

Anyways, what an experience, right? So from one weird anomaly to another, may God bless you, and if God doesn't exist, may you be blessed regardless and enjoy whatever life is.

Atomically, there's nothing to you. If we press onwards beyond electron clouds, protons, neutrons, quarks, it seems nothing but nothingness awaits us. It's all vibrational waves of energy manifesting the realm of the physical - a cosmic giggle, a dance, a celebration.

Chemically, however, you are something, a concoction of weird stuff that induces feelings, emotions, this trip. You're hallucinating from the ingredients that comprise you, forgetting what's before you is a reaction from what's within you, what is you.

Biologically, you're an animal, a three-dimensional being of Earth. Your body is of this planet, this environment. It shares features, DNA, and nature with other earthlings, implying your body isn't a separate spaceship carrying you; it's a force deeply connected with all beings throughout the history of organic life on Earth.

Mentally, you're an intricate web of everything you've ever perceived and more - the mind. You're also an ego. You tell stories, create characters, play out roles. You linguistically format an identity and act according to a script.

Consciously, you're an alien. You dreamwalk and time-warp between dimensions of experience through presence, fantasy and memories. Because of that, there doesn't seem to be a limit to your creativity. You're a descendent of the fantastic imagination.

Ultimately, you make no sense. You're a mystery we cannot rationalise, for we cannot logically refer to anything to explain existence as there's nothing to base our analysis on; for what is there to reference other than the mystery itself?

What we are is what I attempted to explore within this book by philosophising existence. However, I also included poetic, expressive, and independent pieces, as my primary interest was to bleed my mind and soul. Therefore, relevant separate passages follow each topic.

U
N
K
N
O
W
N

/ʌnˈnəʊn/

: mysterious - unsaid.
That which lies beneath the bed of
humanity's linguistically fed illusions.

/JUX

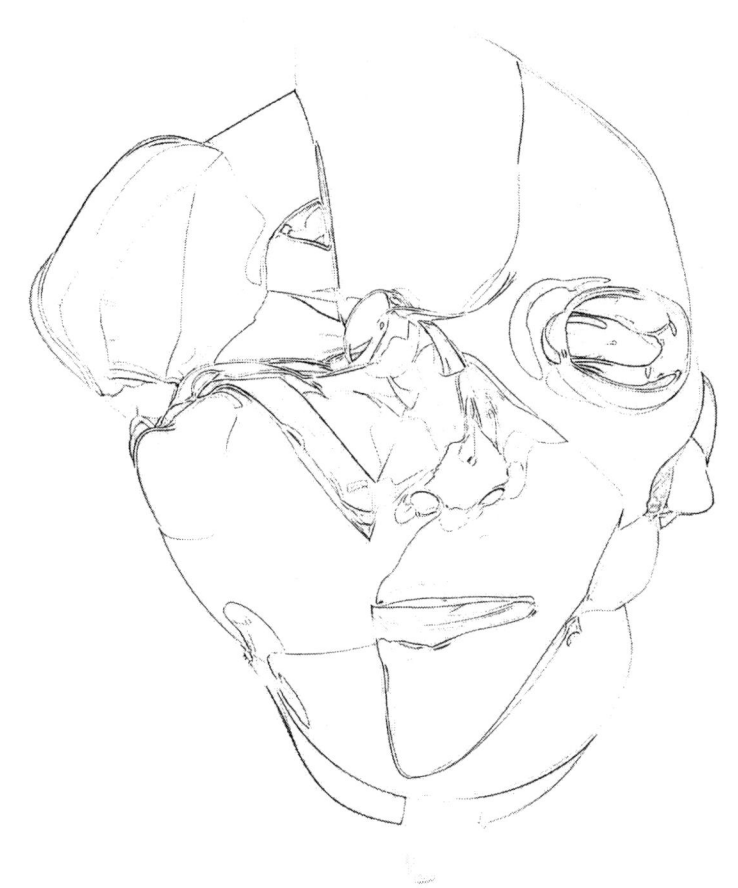

Have you considered what you are, exactly? Seriously, what are you? Seemingly, you've come up from nothing, out of nowhere, with such a troublesome nature to understand in an equally mysterious environment. What is this place? Where are we? Perhaps it's land for dreams - space for the unreal to materialise. However, this doesn't answer the question; it only inspires the need to investigate further for what is matter? Well, it's vibrational energy. But what the hell is that? We can ask more and more forever and ever, for what awaits us at the basis of everything isn't conclusive, and that's quite the laugh.

I remember listening to a recording of Alan Watts, and sometime during his talk, he mentioned it's better suited for us to consider ourselves a verb rather than a noun. Of course, that's a bit of a rebellious act knowing most of us are hellbent on terming ourselves nowadays. However, he suggests nouns are illusory and misconstrue information. Therefore, perhaps we're referring to ourselves incorrectly, as our language cannot accurately represent what and who we are for the reference point we ask questions from isn't legitimate.

When you're thinking, you are a motion of thoughts. The 'I' itself is a thought. Therefore, there is no I who thinks - you don't do this - you are the doing, the thinking. Interestingly, with this in mind, when you consider fundamental philosophical inquiries, such as what we're attempting here, and you question your relation to the universe, you no longer separate yourself from the cosmos with this perspective. You don't consider yourself an independent creation needing explanation; you see your existence as the 'creation.' You're not a separate agent witnessing it - you are what's happening. We attain some sense of our existence with this understanding, even though it's entirely against all common sense.

Do reflect on this, especially if you wish to confront philosophical concerns such as your existence, for what we've collectively accomplished is the actualisation of an illusion by defining what something is by creating something it's not, only to trace all information about what it is back to this mistaken identity - ego.

Understandably, we feel perplexed. Therefore, the question concerning what you are isn't plausible, for what we're questioning doesn't exist, so the question is nonsensical, hence the confusion, the incapability of formulating an answer.

Nevertheless, we know you are here, wherever here is, an ineffable anomaly, reading this, which is just absurd. All events since the beginning, if there were a beginning, provided this opportunity to experience the mind of another through text. The existence and expansion of the universe, which is directly related to the evolution of your consciousness, has you here. Right now, this is where it's all at - for you. However, it becomes puzzling when investigating where you are, for where you are is within your mind, though your mind cannot be found anywhere other than out there, before you, within your art, relationships, style, speech, and interactions. Currently, I'm inside your mind as you read, so we're inside out, outside in, like a dream.

Ultimately, you're conscious, consciousness, the mysterious fundamental property of everything. As you read, understand this to be your ordinary awareness. Beyond this text and your bodily senses lies further information assimilated by your subconscious. However, you are physically, mentally and energetically restricted, causing you to be consciously limited when interacting with the infinite information permeating this field of activity, this domain of experience known as existence. Engulfing you is vast information you're unaware of, within and without, which could alter everything you believe to be true. Therefore, knowing who, what or where you are is paradoxical, for it's momentary, as eventually, you will attain knowledge about yourself and this realm, refuting the understanding you currently have of yourself.

If we know anything at all, it'd be that what we deem to be true now, be it scientific knowledge or religious belief, will soon be remodelled with novel understanding and perspective. The irony of truth is that it's subject to change upon awareness.

To increase understanding through consciousness, you must give

2

up truth, push boundaries, think the unimaginable, shift perspectives and travel through each dimension of the self via introspection. It's the path of enlightenment through the dark. In doing so, your cognisance will expand to take in more than you initially could, for you tweaked your perception, shifted your perspective, and exuviated the self. The result is painful although astounding, benefiting your experience as you live more accurate to your nature.

For example, through this process, I developed the basis of my morality. It became my philosophy to treat all how I'd like to be treated without discrimination. However, I will occasionally fail to practice this without contradiction, hypocrisy, for I am merely human, and acceptance of that allows me to live truly. No matter what, I will be destructive. People will suffer because of me, as will other creatures and the environment supporting my existence. Ironically, by nature, I am a burden to the lives of others, to nature. However, as painful as it is, I favour awareness over ignorance. Therefore, to the best of my conscious ability, I will limit how negatively impactful I am towards others, be they human or non-human.

The decision to live consciously impacts your reality, and your reality is what you're hallucinating. You can stay linguistically drugged by others, confined to a matrix, projecting whatever ideology your culture is pedalling, exploring as far as your language permits, imprisoning your imagination to the limitations of truth, perhaps unknowingly converting your reality into a bad trip; this world into a cruel jest. Or, you can reclaim your human experience by surrendering to the unknown, releasing your mind, learning about yourself, going a bit mad and getting wild with existence by philosophising. And don't be afraid to philosophise. This realm, this space, it's anyone's guess, and by nature, you are both an explorer and mystery, the embodiment of a dream.

You are what I am - unknown in thought though known in presence. Whatever your deal is as an entity, force, energy - the

same applies to me. Our linguistic character deludes that.
Although I philosophise our existence for entertainment and joy,
paradoxically, words only thicken the veil.

It's awkward trying to form meaningful friendships if you've consciously deviated from cultural normality and embraced an unorthodox, eccentric lifestyle from self-exploration. You hardly fit in anywhere. Your peers' activities, vernacular, and conversations are lacklustre; they don't stimulate your heart, mind, or soul. And each to their own, this isn't a 'holier than thou' attitude, it's just - you're so mindfully and spiritually elsewhere that it's hard to engage.

You're an alien at social events, and you only attend them because the loneliness of remaining isolated can be overly depressing, particularly the absence of having a sincere, romantic connection. That hurts most, not being touched, held or sexually desired by someone who dances to the same tune as you. It often results in forming relationships that barely involve real love.

Instead, you're either continuously settling for individuals who don't share the same intellectual thirst as yourself, for they're disinterested in entertaining the esoteric fields of spiritual activity or philosophic thought you consciously enjoy exploring. Or, you find yourself intimately involved with people who use spirituality and abstract thinking to circumvent trauma that occasionally surfaces throughout the relationship, dragging you into emotionally tiresome circumstances. Either way, you concede the price to be paid for conscious expansion in an unconscious society is a social and romantic life.

So, you've formed an interest in spirituality, psychology, and philosophy, though you're unsure where to begin. I assume you underwent a significant life event that pulled down the curtain of reality, or perhaps you've always been curious, wanting a sneak peek underneath. Whatever the case, you've acknowledged the mystery that is your existence. However, an audience of faces has now greeted you, shouting non-duality, shadow work, enlightenment, dark night of the soul, kundalini activation, third-eye, ego death, higher-self, Nietzsche, Jung, and other names, practices, books, topics, studies or experiments.

Consequently, you're overwhelmed by the unconventional information, being told by said people to read this or do that while reevaluating your most stubborn truths and beliefs. Unfortunately, what I have to say on this matter is only further noise, adding to the line of people directing you. But what I suggest is to go a simplistic yet more direct route. Rather than immediately entertaining what everyone is saying, take moments of your day, perhaps during your work break, to sit alone outside. Slowly source your mystery at your pace through introspection, conscious attention and presence. Reflect upon your thoughts; question why you have such an opinion or viewpoint. See if you can alter your perspective to acquire a newfound understanding. Patiently, do this indefinitely. That is philosophy and psychology at play.

Afterwards, attempt to entertain a moment of inner silence by watching the world. Listen to the surrounding noise, the cars, people, insects and birds. Feel your environment, where you stand or sit, the breeze pressing upon your skin. Ground your being with the collective happening. If you have a conversation with another, maybe while purchasing lunch, try to interact human to human, mystery to mystery. See yourself within them. That's spirituality. Ultimately, take your time. Remember, these studies and practices concern your existence, so who better to inquire and learn from than yourself?

Trying to find yourself is the reason you feel lost. It's a deceptive pursuit. Who's looking? Who's going to find who? You? There, you're found.

I know you haven't felt like your usual self lately; especially with the recent events of the world. I know you feel off-balance, out of place, and you can't quite understand why. It's not an entirely unfamiliar state, you've been here many times, but something is different; there's a sense of uncertainty like you're unsure what to do or where to go. It's okay to admit that frightens you; I won't pretend I can't relate to such a state. Though, because I can, I feel as if I should offer you my thoughts.

The unknown is precisely where we should be if we desire to grow as humans. It is within those periods of inner-tribulations that we unearth knowledge about ourselves, an understanding that is not of words, but of feeling, of acquiring a sense of 'spiritual' clarity through rebirth. If you wake to read this, upon a new day, you can regather yourself by paradoxically letting go of a previous you. There is no place for you to be other than this puzzling, incomprehensible moment we call now where all comes into being through forms of complexity and pure art.

It's a matter of no longer trying so hard to control the uncontrollable, which is what we're living within. It's chaotic - and trying to straighten it out as if you could determine your path is like thinking that squinting your eyes will help you understand something more clearly.

You're unsure of yourself, what you want or where to go. However, you don't want to be left behind, left to age but not grow, exist though not live, so you follow. You go along with everyone else. You force yourself to entertain environments and individuals that soulfully feel unrelatable. You sacrifice your individuality through cultural rituals by participating in conventional activities to acquire a sense of belonging. You become someone contrary to your truth, living within a matrix awaiting a moment of completion, fulfilment, space in which you say, "ah, I've finally made it." It's not going to happen. Look, the secret to knowing yourself, what you want or where to go is to stop looking. Once you do that, you'll suddenly appear. For this whole attitude of finding oneself is to circle a room endlessly in search of no one.

You do not hate yourself. A collection of thoughts forming an identity hates an image elicited from the fallacious ideas assimilated as self. The real you, what you're too culturally drugged to realise, is beyond such a trivial and irrational perception.

/ɪɡəʊ, ɛɡəʊ/

———•••◆•••———

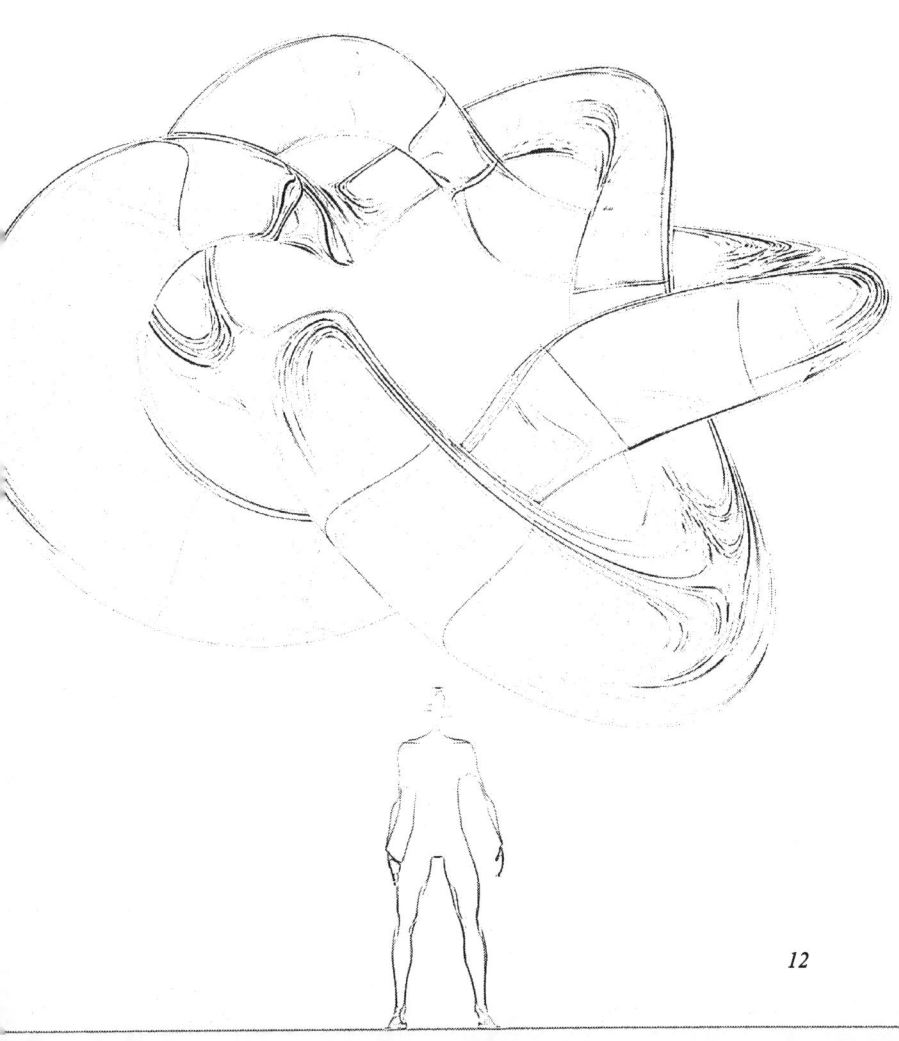

Metaphysically speaking, the ego is a linguistically manifested identity utilised as a reference point to consciously comprehend the external. This is what 'I' think, 'I' see, 'I' believe - this is who 'I' am. Ego is routing consciousness through thoughts - every thought you have post-feeling is ego.

Ego holds no real substance, meaning what you think to be true doesn't, or your identity, or reality, thus the illusion. A witty person will consider the contradiction that based on this understanding, this is a thought and therefore lacks validity, proving it incorrect. However, it's proven valid in its undoing, for both ego and this understanding cease once you stop thinking. That is the state of meditation.

If your ego does not know itself to be illusory, you're bound to be played by others, particularly your culture. You will go about life filtering this experience through such a shallow pool of understanding. See, notice how you and your world are a matter of your lexicon, for as you look around, you will refer all that you see to an internal dictionary; a dictionary given to you by culture. Therefore, what's before you isn't what's really there, as what's perceived is first referenced to your language, then culture, then ideology, and so forth until the external thing you see is entirely altered into something other than its raw form. Therefore, tragically, when most people come across their reflection, they perceive themselves in words, overlooking how phenomenal they naturally are.

Consider the situation of relocating a fourteenth-century orthodox Middle Eastern man and a sixteenth-century orthodox Irishman into the same room. You'd have two humans sharing the same space, comprised of the same source, yet living dimensions apart. However, if you found them as they were born, time-travelled to the present, and raised them under your house, in your country, in your culture, with your religion and language, their reality would hardly differ from one another until perhaps they became adults. That is the connection between ego, language and reality. "So if I'm not me, these thoughts, who am I?" Well, ironically, let's think about that. Right now, you're flowing, occurring, along with everything. Your being is a continuation of the grand cosmic giggle. Your heart is beating as blood circulates, nerves tingle, cells duplicate, atoms vibrate, planets form, stars die, space expands - you are this happening which your ego has no involvement in because it doesn't exist in the first place. If you don't believe me, don't think, feel; feel down into your core in solitude until you're so far within that your thoughts are unheard, and you unearth a self that is much more us than 'I.'

The solution to almost all of our problems is simply a change in perspective. However, no one wants to give up the mental space they egotistically occupy, clinging onto their culture, beliefs, truths, doing whatever it takes, be it through greed or violence, to maintain their illusory sense of self.

Our whole problem as a civilisation is ego, and we will largely remain mentally unwell until the education system guides children into understanding the identity crisis that dictates their adult life. For every societal difficulty and world conflict caused by humans, from the commoner to the elitist, results from a mind lacking the insight or care to differentiate between the illusory character and the self. Racism, bullying, violence, greed, corruption, and war, this is all ego attempting to maintain form by deforming consciousness. It disrupts direct connection, starves the soul and induces loneliness. If we have any interest in elevating humanity for the better, then ego death is necessary. As a civilisation, we must know the illusion. Unfortunately, however, we're in a mess, as it's probably too great of an economic problem to introduce meditative practices because self-aware individuals cannot be automated to continue feeding this system directing civilisation, for someone mentally, physically, and spiritually healthy has no place in this society or economy, as what are you to do with them? What are you going to sell them? They don't want your drugs; they don't enjoy your fast food; they don't need your psychology or therapy. They are a maverick, 'weirdos,' and need to be shunned, silenced, kept under control or they risk influencing the mass with their wholesome lifestyle, destabilising the matrix.

I believe deep down, we know ego to be fictitious. Hence, we subconsciously doubt our existence and feel out of place because we primarily operate from a lie. We say we don't know who we are and panic, begin contributing to a culture of sourcing identity through attention or over-consumption for a sense of feeling real. We linguistically imprint ourselves everywhere, along with our image, to be seen, heard, and felt, evident through the popularity and use of social media. It's an existential crisis, and we've been undergoing it for an exceptionally lengthy period. Generation after generation collectively manifests this anxiety; it's the unknowing root of many decisions. War reveals it well. Humans do not wage war for land, power, control or conflict of ideology; that's a surface-level interpretation as we intuitively know there's nothing here to attain and no one here to possess anything. We all die. No, humans fight because they're unsure of themselves; they kill because they're uncomfortable with being. The misunderstanding of who we are promotes these unhealthy mentalities, observed throughout all human interactions and interests. Our diets, intimacy, and relationships detail where we're consciously at with the comfort of ourselves, particularly our impermanence, for a person at odds with themselves is at odds with others. We're allowing the mental stress of establishing ourselves to deliver a sense of relief which is the cause of the mental stress. It's a vicious cycle.

I don't believe the human mind can handle the body. It's too multidimensional, too alien that unless one occasionally exists the mind and reconnects with the body or perpetually remains distracted with addictions, they will seek a way out through destruction. The ego is the perpetrator of that destruction, attempting to tunnel a way out from the intensity of consciousness.

Although, I pity humanity. There was never a guide for us detailing how to handle this level of consciousness, and we've overlooked the effect this has had on our psyche. I believe we're traumatised, frightened by what we discovered and tragically reacting like any animal would if it were subjected to the same depths of the unknown through consciousness. Perhaps fundamental truths and beliefs are how we deal with this trauma amplified by knowing death. We try to get comfortable with a perspective before lying down and dying. It's a self-comfort practice, hence the role of the ego, a voice soothing us with prosocial lies until we die. We're gently running our fingers through our hair with whatever truth, saying, "shh, you'll be okay." And fair enough, I think we accidentally, innocently, became aware of something we weren't ready for, and the PTSD is horrifyingly everywhere.

Perhaps the same can be said for why we tell stories, obsess with progression, strip the land bare, and feel the need to explore the yet to be known. We don't do it for survival, curiosity or enjoyment, but out of fear; we're terrified of what's coming. The moment we consciously evolved to comprehend our mortal predicament to this degree, we've been running away, stomping over everything in our path in the name of civilisation and evolution. Human history is a stampede. We're a species attempting to outrun the inevitable. Consequently, ego emerged as a mediator, a voice, inventing characters such as 'God' to ironically calm our predicament as caged animals being lowered into the alien ocean of our mind. That is why if we don't create a stable relationship by instilling meditative practices, we'll rattle the cage, disturb the water, and sink from the sheer gravity of our mental situation.

A great place to achieve this is reconnecting with Mother Nature, for no ego survives days spent in her presence. Her temper stips you naked of your arrogance; her elements drown your thoughts until that linguistic, cultured parasite exits your psyche, and you remember your place in this world.

The following examples outline the extremities of certain egos. It's not a psychological telling detailing mentalities through extensive research but rather a simple expression from observation of my social surroundings. Do not read as if it informs you what you are. It's to display the coding of ego, and how it overrides the mind to present a character so inauthentic such detail below can be recorded from pattern recognition.

Ego#1

• The most common. Doesn't think much; rarely independently sources an opinion. Develops consumerist qualities to fill the void and follows the dominant perspective/lifestyle mindlessly. Life or 'truth' goes no further than their culture. Easily manipulated, especially by ego#2.

Ego#1.2

• #1.2 is what can become of #1 if exposed to consciousness-expanding information, such as a near-death experience, spiritual encounter or assimilation of profound knowledge. Unfortunately, they tend to find themselves lost due to living blindly for so long, struggling to discontinue moving with the herd. They stagnate with plenty of questions, as answering them for themselves is foreign. What's best for them is to be reborn again.

Ego#1.3

• The same as #1, but due to favourable circumstances, such as economic and geographic positioning, the ego gives way to narcissism, greed, overconsumption - extreme self-indulgence. Ego#1 can become #1.3 overnight due to lacking integrity established by self-exploration. The type to leave their marriage upon winning the lottery. They have a protagonist of the universe mentality and rarely entertain the thought practice of seeing themselves within the external.

Ego#2

• Intellectually pretentious merely due to having a shrewd mind; everyone is stupid bar themselves. They are opinionated and unable to disagree without stating their thoughts. More likely to remain within the boundaries of logic as they lack creativity, for they fear self-exploration, partly because they don't like themselves. Consequently, they are more likely to suffer from harmful addictions for escape. Usually cannot stand people hosting ego#3 because they find them too spurious. Can be incredibly pessimistic.

Ego#3

• A sensitive, insecure thinker with a fragile identity. They seek the alternative for a sense of belonging, understanding, meaning, and attention to avoid directly dealing with the underlying trauma. Very out there, illogical, self-righteous, and contradictory due to lacking mental stability. Ironically egocentric.

Ego#4

• Methodical thinkers; systematic. Similar to #2, but more informed than intelligent. They assimilate information primarily through statistics and research rather than felt experience. The world is straightforward to them as it goes no further than the prevailing reality. They project a lot and misconstrue contrary views they cannot make sense of, as it doesn't fit within their boxed mind. Befriends or idolises ego#2, sometimes relying on them to express their thoughts. Also cannot stand ego#3. Usually, Western men channel consciousness through this ego.

Ego#5

> • Independent overthinkers. They analyse everything, preferably from afar, echoing thoughts, inducing severe anxiety, and therefore, rarely socialise due to the overwhelming information ingested. They become a shut-in if their cognitive habits aren't dealt with through suitable mindful practices. Worse, the ego can eventuate into a character of extreme destruction. However, if they overcome this, they're capable of intellectual greatness.

Ego#6

> • Continually projects and misconstrues others as they live within their world. Most likely suffers from an inferiority complex, casting thoughts over a wall protecting their unacknowledged insecurities. They think primarily about themselves and are so mentally convoluted that even facts or reality cannot penetrate their mind. Rarely, if ever, admits to being wrong.

Ego#0

> • Uneducated, uncultivated, little to no thoughts. There isn't much to them; no one at home. If they're cognitively debilitated and emotionally disconnected, lacking consciousness, they struggle to develop a conscience, becoming harmful toward society. However, if they're intelligent, conscious, self-reflective, and self-taught, they can emerge as artists forming a unique ego producing novel ideas as their mind is unrestrained.

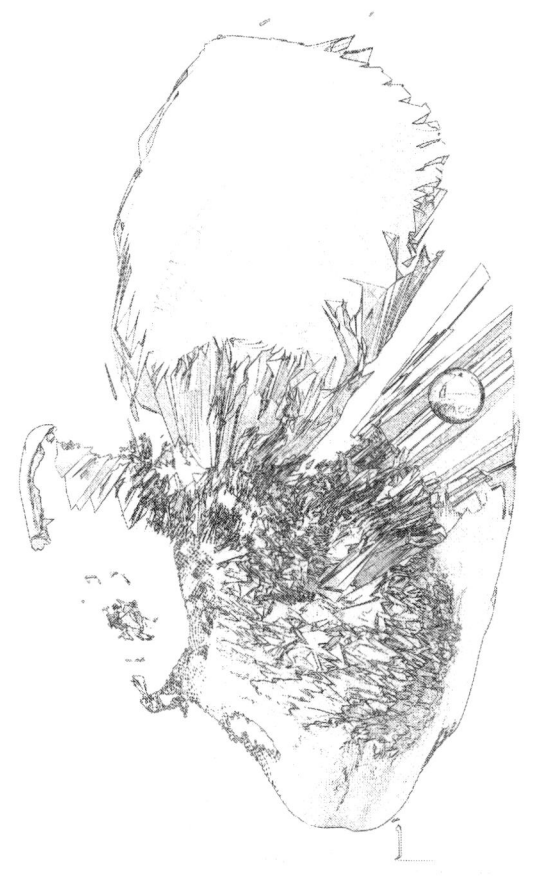

There is no need to abandon ego unless you intend to meditate or be without any thought. Instead, the ego should treat ego like pottery and shape itself to serve the body and soul.

If I were egoless, 'I' wouldn't be here, for I'd be the here in which I wasn't, for I was 'I.'

Modern society, what a performance.

Who am I? Who's asking? Me. Who's that? Exactly. What? Huh? You're talking. No, I'm listening. Who is? You. The voice in my head? Yes. But that's me? No, that's me. Who?

*No, no, wrong!! *pssch-pop, burp*
My opinion, my opinion, cite some source, TV on,
background news, scrolling, consuming, don't like
something, state objection, argue with stranger, pull back
recliner, eat farmed animal, take medication, walk around
as the centre of the universe, sleep, repeat.*

Attention, attention, listen, I'm real, listen to me, me, me, this is
what I believe. No, you're wrong, I'm right, I'm real! See?
Watch, watch, look, look, this is what I am, something,
something, here, there, you watching? I know, I know, my truth,
it's true, I know! It's me, you, him, her, they, them, it, define me
please, tell me I'm real; I'm real!

My guess to what we ultimately mean by thought is the final product of a response. Information enters the womb of our cognition via our senses, which we creatively and intellectually dress, adding layers of symbols from the wardrobe of language, forming the thinker, 'I,' a base point for consciousness to create reality. However, if we cannot find suitable attire for translation, the thought remains naked in the form of a feeling.

See, I've partially entered your mind right now. Respectfully, I'll leave my shoes at the door because I mean well, but being linguistically dressed appropriately, I can infiltrate and assist in clothing your thoughts, influencing your identity and, therefore, reality, so long as you identify as the thinker. That is why people feel personally attacked when their thoughts are challenged, as they don't want to change clothes, for they'll lose their sense of self. It's hilarious. Look at me; I'm walking around this mysterious, unlocatable space of yours. Mind if I sit here? Pun intended. I'm just having fun. It's the play of words, which has no substance compared to what's unsaid, to these raw, undressed thoughts you have here, behind the wardrobe, your intuition and love.

There isn't much difference in ego between an insecure person and a narcissist. Both are overly hung up on the idea they have of themselves.

/ˈNEITʃə/

Underlying this physical realm, propagating life, is the mysterious phenomenon identified as Mother Nature. Through our perception, we know it as that which happens itself, be it cause or effect, from the gravitational waves disturbing space-time to the ocean waves of Earth to your heart beating; nature is everything. You are, at the core of your being, this force. However, ego differs, consciously redirecting your mind toward a linguistic viewpoint that overlooks a significant portion of your existence while presenting an identity to reference as you. Philosophically, we can still see this as nature, as it's eventuated here, within us, yet we'll distinguish a difference for clarity of self.

If we're sincere about understanding ourselves, we must factor in our surroundings. We must realise our intrinsic connection with nature, for our environment has as much to do with our being as our organs. If one seeks to benefit themselves, they must care for their habitat and those within it, for we share a symbiotic relationship, and part of the self resides in the external. That implies to be selfish, truly, is to focus on being selfless, for you cannot prosper as a healthy individual while simultaneously destroying the space in which you grow. Like a plant, you cannot flourish if you tarnish your soil, block out the sun, destroy the land upon which you stand or shun all forms of communication with your soul because your soul is indeed before you in the eyes of others, within rocks and water. Throughout all of nature is a candid reflection of what comprises us; the strength of the mountains, the rage of volcanic eruptions, the mystery of sea caves, the tranquillity of death and the chaos of life.

I have lost myself time and time again in the world of man, only to find myself in the heart of nature.

Yet, as we know, we have a suicidal attitude. We're on edge. We oppose each other environmentally, politically, and spiritually. We hardly get along with anything external or internal. Our mentality is self-destructive, our activity is a knife held to our throat. One who claims this attitude to be a matter of progression or survival to justify the situation is a pretender because what is meant by progression? What in the world are we trying to do as a species? Where are we trying to go? Naturally, everything is already here if happiness is our intent. There's no need for anything else. Survival? We look sickly dressed like this, boxed in dull houses, offices, vehicles, fighting the afternoon traffic. Prolonging one's life at the expense of the soul is no life at all. And evolution? I'm unsure if anyone understands what evolution means other than what we've defined as a process of natural selection. I wouldn't recommend limiting yourself to the evolution or survival model either. Entertain it, sure, but it's intellectually debilitating to refer to this perspective for every argument. It may even influence cognitive habits that overlook crucial alternative knowledge, for you'll subconsciously filter information like picking suitable *Jenga* pieces to hold this model together. I wince when I realise someone's philosophical position strictly revolves around living a longer life; what kind of viewpoint is that? No, we have no idea, and seemingly, no collective interest in pausing and reflecting on this momentous matter. As for the intent of Mother Nature's existence and growth of life on Earth, I'm unsure. I'm not going to lie and con you into believing some idea of mine, but I will philosophise what I intuitively feel may be true.

I think nature is intelligent by how we recognise intelligence. She's not entirely arbitrary, merely allowing evolution with its chaotic and violent manner to determine what survives by chance of mutations and adaptation to a novel climate. Perhaps it's biased, but we're too weird for that. I don't see the depth of our intellect and creative abilities or their relevance necessary to overcoming the conditions of a particular environment. For what reason would we need to fall in love? Or sing? Or dance?

From an analytical perspective, there's no sense in moving like that in a universe of disorder, but we can't stop ourselves from dancing. We're in a realm of such death and destruction, you would think our around-the-clock objective would be survival, yet when that beat starts, away we flow. You could suggest a psychological purpose, but I mentioned depth. We create and partake in alien-like activities; meditating in the rain would have sufficed if the aim was mental health. So if this comes natural, it's inherently 'meaningful.' We play music and throw our bodies around while making noise because Mother Nature intended for us to do that. We are like children entertaining our parents Saturday night because we are more suited to artistic expression than running stock markets or managing retail stores. Therefore, our existence as a species, the meaning of our evolution by choice of Gaia, is perhaps a matter of celebration, of seeing just how expressive we can get by turning ourselves inside out. That itself may be the dream of the universe. However, we have strayed. We've chosen the wrong attire under false guidance spread by confused and fear-inducing ideology and rocked up to the celebration of life over-dressed.

As another idea, perhaps planets are aware of their demise from the inevitable failure of their star, and through the guidance of nature, these giants organically incarnate with intention to evolve into an interstellar travelling species. With this notion, earthlings are the embodiment of earth, coming into being from the sunlight penetrating her fertile body. Mother Nature, therefore, acts as a midwife, assisting with cultivating space to develop such a kind. We, to some degree, fit that description. Understandably, we're nowhere near the possibility of travelling the solar system, let alone outside, but we possess relatable characteristics for this task. We're obsessed with exploring the unknown, evident throughout our history in traversing multiple terrains as we mapped the world, and within our academic pursuits, mathematical advancements, cosmological discoveries, scientific experiments, the expectancy of alien contact and the imagination. We are seemingly, inherently driven forward or pulled towards the unknown. I recognise this within myself through philosophy, spirituality, and self-exploration. Although I'm not biologically equipped with the awareness or the intellect to understand the universe, I am fitted with a heart and an imagination that begs me to try. If this is our purpose, it also implies a responsibility towards cultivating life, not destroying it, for we cannot explore something if it's no longer there.

Lastly, maybe we are destroyers, destined to blow ourselves up along with this entire planet. After all, Mother Nature is catastrophic in her ways of cultivation, and if we're a matter of her dream, then disregarding the possibility we are volcanic eruptions, tsunamis, or astroids embodied in the flesh is unreasonable. We could be here as an extinction event, maybe the final one that'll shoot DNA out into space or be the cause of an explosion so mighty the space this planet occupies will burn the core of a star. Modern humanity is destructive. We exchange trees for houses, forests for roads, lakes for airports, land for shopping centres, mountains for temples - all in the name of the development of civilisation. However, towards what end? I don't think we create nuclear weapons for potential warfare. That is a lie we tell ourselves as we pretend to care about politics, the growth of tyrants, or the protection for the continuation of existence in a mortal plane. That's all shallow play; humans getting about with ideologies, defining themselves by it, pretending it has any relevance to the universe. Nobody, truly, beneath everything they egoically are, believes that. I would question whether the real reason we're obsessed with such physics is that behind our ordinary consciousness, ingrained into our nature, is a desire to kill ourselves through total annihilation. We want to die, like artists, splattering ourselves until we're out there as art. And if this all did indeed begin with a bang, then maybe that nature flows on through us, and we're here to make another big bang.

Whatever our meaning, if any, I feel more aligned with celebrating. My desire to dance, sing, laugh and love is too intrinsic to my being to think otherwise. Although darkness is relevant, it's not prevalent. Mother Nature bears fangs, claws, blood drooling from her mouth though her body is that of a Goddess. No matter the mental or chemical influences, we can consciously decide what part of her we predominantly feature.

The relationship between nature and consciousness is fascinating, although perplexing. I humorously think it'd be easier to make sense of existence if physicality was non-existent, for I have a much better time philosophising my mind than I do with this realm. I entertain consciousness as somewhat of a diaphanous 'thing' infinitely filling every dimension of space with its mysterious property. However, on the other hand, nature is a disturbing alien force freely moving across dimensions or universes that begins to make a fuss upon interaction with consciousness, vibrating, pulling together particles, energy, and meshing weird ingredients until organic life forms. So this universe may have once been an individual consciousness dreaming until Mother Nature infiltrated this space and began extracting agents, be them celestial, planetary, animal, insect or what have you, for whatever reason, if any, into what is meant by the physical.

If you have the curiosity and patience, nature has the lessons and wisdom.

To clean the mind, all one must do is occasionally dirty themselves in nature. To be bitten by insects, bathed in sweat, washed by a waterfall and dressed by sunlight.

At least once a week, I recommend you go for a walk, find a tree, sit not with a friend or book, but only yourself, and open pages of your mind in silence.

Whenever I'm experiencing mental or emotional pain, I sit before the sun, with my hands in the earth and my feet on the grass, saying "heal" before gently humming. I do this for as long as need be, and after some time, my mind settles, my heart strengthens - my spirit rejuvenates.

I'm a tad insane. Mad with wonder. Slightly weird. I debate God, question truth, fear no demon, no secret, no mystery. I'm a harmless suicidal simple living lunatic in love with nature and baffled by existence.

The reason I love Mother Nature so much is that she doesn't tell a lie. She's entirely there, in all her horror and beauty, hiding nothing, unlike man, whose world is a collection of falsehoods.

It can be deadly to embellish nature poetically, for she is not all roses and valleys; she is ravenous and bloody. You are too. You can deny that in your place of comfort, play the character, name and job title, but there's an animal within, bearing the fangs of the jungle from which you came. And the longer you neglect it, the longer you continue running away from home, from Mother Nature, the more hungry this creature grows, ready to consciously consume you whole upon any moment of disorder.

Exit the world, enter the wild, dirty your body, wash your soul, dissolve your ego, reveal the illusion, meet yourself.

/BᴅDI/

---◆---

46

Look at us, limbs, face, organs, skin, bones, hilarious. The physical realm is weird and paradoxical, for solid isn't solid atomically speaking. You'd hardly be physical, if at all, were you to condense your being by vacuuming all the space comprising you. What absurdity, right? Yet physics avers by offering such profundity from studying matter at a quantum level. It flouts common sense because, look, here we are, stamping our feet, shaking hands, touching the external. However, everything 'physical' is fundamentally frequency waves of vibrational energy. You've probably heard or read that a million times, bannered everywhere within the spiritual community. We are this property of matter vibrating as form. But where does this property come from? Let's trace it backwards.

Arguably, energy is continuous; it gives way to further energy. It passes on information, provoking a reaction, and influencing shape. So the energy comprising you today, arranging atoms, structuring your body, functions as it has many times before bar the slight transformations from novelty; hence your overall form. Thus, it's wise to consider what presence you wish to entertain within your space, be it external through social means or internal such as diet and sex. Whether you're conscious of it or not, it will impact you, as behind our ordinary perception, intricate activity is energetically taking place, which involves transferring information. You can realise this within your movement, for energy through movement is a process of sharing knowledge over generations and species. When I raise my arm, I connect with the lineage of many earthlings. When I dance, I flow with my ancestors. They're right there, within, as a voice, feeling, premonition, intuition, guiding me towards a greater understanding of self. Walking, as an example, isn't simply walking; it's an enormous feat and historically meaningful in biology. Every conscious step interacts with our forebears. It symbolises their perseverance, for the action is a practice innately embedded energetically within humanity. It represents our will to overcome unfavourable odds by evolving.

If you're capable, go for a walk daily. It doesn't matter where or

*for how long - engage with the art of mind over matter. Its
psychological benefits are unmatched.*

To understand what I'm proposing, consider energy as the web of
space and time, manipulating space and time, passing on
information throughout each physical manifestation. Perhaps that's
what's occurring with people who believe they convey with the
departed. Ghosts, spirits, demons, dead mentors - are not foreign,
external and separate; they exist to some degree through the
ancient energy giving us form for that same energy once partially
gave form to those entities. However, our brain habitually projects
them into our realm through the dominant senses, ironically for
means of comprehension. Psychologically unexplained 'evil' could
be somewhat clarified with this perspective; that negative or
traumatic energy persists from one life to another, as displayed
within a malign individual who proceeds to commit horrid acts
even though their psyche is seemingly intact. If this is anywhere
near to being accurate regarding the origin and essence of energy,
we can take it further to the universe's formation. Whatever all of
this is, be it the love child of Mother Nature and consciousness,
understanding it may be a matter (pun intended) of deeply feeling
your energy.

The wisest among us are only repeating what you already know.

To understand yourself through the body, you must develop a
healthy relationship between your masculinity and femininity, for
they are the penetrative and receptive forces behind introspection.
If they are imbalanced and unsupportive of one another, you will
not get far unearthing your truth, for if you reject self-examination
by refusing to acknowledge your emotions, nullifying your
femity, you won't comprehend your being. Similarly, if you were
to avoid all confrontation that may arise challenging realisations,
such as surfacing a suppressed memory or investigating your
beliefs by interrogating any bias through channelling your
masculinity, you won't make sense of yourself. Therefore, it is
crucial to nourish these two forces and interact with them.
Otherwise, you have no choice but to rely on outside sources for

definition and truth, which is contradictory for the subject of inquiry is you. You are the mystery, so engage with your entirety. Learn to connect with what comprises you for self-understanding.

As a heterosexual male, dominantly masculine, I remember dreaming of this beautiful, naked woman when I was around fifteen, even though I hadn't honestly seen a naked woman before. Of course, I knew the anatomy, but my dream detailed her so raw, so true, it was like I was looking at something I shouldn't be seeing. She was ethereal, nothing I had ever seen in this realm. And I remember staring, experiencing this strange feeling as I turned into an animal, only to then have my way with her. I penetrated her with my ugliness, my weak, premature energy spoiling her nature. It took years for me to make sense of that dream. I made nothing of it as a teenager, but it stuck with me, and as an adult, I realised how meaningful this dream was to my puberty and transition out of boyhood. I dreamt of this female to better understand the feminine to become a man; it acted as a lesson to inform me of what I am and need to do regarding interacting with my inner-femininity. Had I failed to unearth such insight, I'd have a child's mentality within a man's body, repressed and imbalanced from my ignorance and arrogance. That would lead to unhealthy masculinity, influencing me to negatively affect the external and internal environments I inhabit, for I rejected my maternal side and deprived myself of self-nourishment.

See, I think our mothers leave us all with a maternal-like force that propagates the maturation of our emotions and energy. However, it's common for men to cut themselves off from this internal force as they follow social and cultural customs to become a man, not realising this rejection causes them to remain a boy. We're all birthing ourselves constantly, but disempowering 'her' within us deforms our ability to develop into adults. So that woman in my dream was my femininity, and ever since I accepted her, my masculinity has benefited. The message is the same for overly feminine individuals who abhor their masculinity. They become overwhelmingly sensitive to a degree in which they significantly increase the odds of becoming shut-ins, for the world is too much to handle. They hide away, fearing even the most minor social environments as they're too stimulated, too receptive energetically within their immediate space. That leads to anxiety and depression because they don't have a balanced relationship with their masculinity which would offer perseverance through the strength of penetration. To go forward and onwards with might, overcoming outside noise, doubt, and anxiety.

Mentally and spiritually, I feel ever-expanding. My body has limits; I don't. Kill me, sure, but nothing, not an injury, human, demon, god or time itself can break my will or soul because I overcame an indescribably dark period long ago. I should have trembled, collapsed, hid in the corner of my room, back against a wall-turned-mouth, consumed by anxiety. But I stood, I grew, like a flame, I moved, enlightening my space. It's my masculinity; I feel like a powerful force with nothing to prove or do but internally expand with light. I'm a freak, well-disciplined, and frankly unafraid of what I am and can become.

What I'm philosophically proposing may seem outrageous. I understand that; I'm as sceptical as they come. However, don't immediately brush this off as far-fetched. Debate, question, philosophise, for we are oblivious to the foundation of our being as we see primarily through thoughts, contaminating what's perceived with ego and, therefore, overlook our happening as well as take it all for granted, resulting in a tremendous loss of self-understanding. We misunderstand what it means to be as we are, for we only go as far as a name, nationality, culture, race, occupation, and birthdate. And sadly, we become so toxic towards ourselves, especially our physicality.

There was a time petty thoughts dominated my perception. I wasn't comprehending just how majestic I am to be here physically, materialised with such complex, wondrous features. My body is trying its best, and I was deluded by culture to think of it as ugly. I'm sure there have been times when you've shared the same thought towards yourself. It's such a negative perspective that induces self-torture, for it can influence habits of vigorously altering one's appearance to suit modern beauty standards. We present ourselves with the sincerity of finding self-worth through the judgement and opinions of others. How horrible. I mean, what or who in the world do we find ugly? What do we even mean by the word ugly? Understandably, instinctual factors biologically affect our feelings of attraction, such as reproduction reasons. However, our attitude toward 'beauty' is far more convoluted than that. When defining attractiveness, we factor in weird physical expectations and demands and respond emotionally troubled if they're not met, sometimes going as far as surgery.

There's something so beautiful about someone willing to openly show just how ugly they are.

Beauty is novelty, which is what you've embodied. You have a body, it's unique - an atomical singularity. You're materialising from vibrating energy like nothing has before in the known universe, including all of your supposed imperfect features. You're magic made flesh, and if we're going to use the word ugly to make sense of ourselves, then let's be reasonable and define it as a term denoting the unshakeable unholy attributes of any organism because I cannot rationalise its relevance to the body. With that in mind, you're as ugly as I am, and I know this because we're of the same stuff. I know what you are, what it's like being this peculiar creature. Sure, perhaps not specifically in detail with certain variations, but I know enough that I can't take you seriously without bursting into laughter. Look at us; I'm practically you just over here, making a different face. I know about the cheekiness, selfishness, wants, fears and dreams. I know all of our secrets, and I can't help but love you because of that.

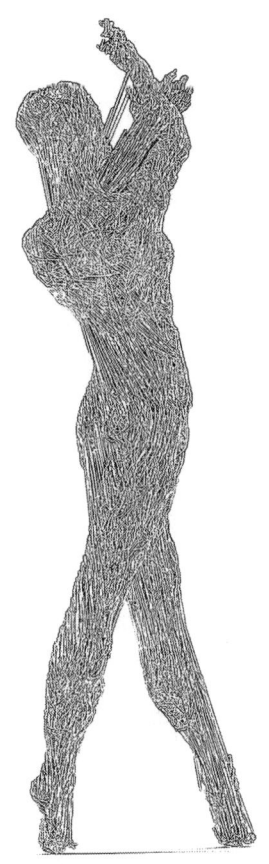

When I was younger, if I had an event to attend, I'd spend every free hour pacing the hallway of my house, repeatedly revisiting the bathroom mirror to tweak my image. Then, most of the time, when the moment came to leave, I'd break down, retreat, and spend the next few days isolated from any reflective object, including people. If I somehow made it out and socialised, I'd over-analyse the facial expressions and body actions of others, observing even the most minor eye movements, questioning whether they were judging or mocking my appearance. Now, however, I gawk in amazement, laugh and show gratitude. "I love you," I tell myself, my body, because the human anatomy is undeniably phenomenal. I realise this whenever I consciously see myself, for I understand energy will never materialise again precisely as I have today, as this unreal form, which is remarkable.

Sometimes I forget I'm a primate. I lose it in laughter when I remember. My ape-like features, limbs, nature, getting about writing philosophy and poetry. Look at me. Hilarious.

When I think about the most beautiful people I've met, those who attracted my heart, they appear to me in form of feeling, sound and movement. It's their ambience, their energy my memory treasures, not their body.

My heartbeat is all the inspiration I need.

/lʌv/

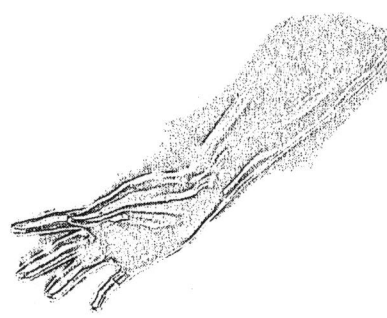

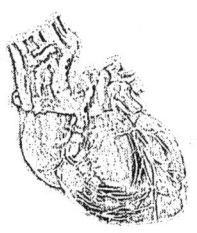

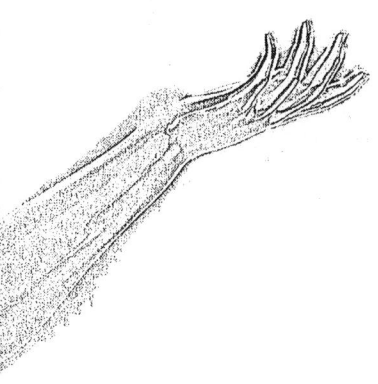

Love is often referred to as a feeling. It comes about from within as a realisation, an epiphany that you're not alone, you're not the only anomaly vibrating on a particular frequency - there's someone just as weird and absurd as you.

If I love you, what I mean is I sincerely appreciate your happening and deeply admire your nature. It's a reaction of respect and gratitude toward your energy, mind, and soul because you remind me of my unspeakable self. That's it. There's nothing else to it, no expectations or demands. Just wow, it's a pleasure to experience your presence. However, I wonder if love is more than a feeling, perhaps a force detailing our identity with more depth and accuracy than any language we speak. For what exactly is this force? Why is it that we humans, if we're fortunate, meet another to such a degree of completion? Many people reduce love to a biological explanation, referencing chemical properties contributing to a dramatic psychological projection for means of survival. But that's an oversimplified model, usually operated by those who are seemingly intelligent though afraid of exploration and vulnerability, probably due to trauma regarding love or attraction. I think it is far more than that. It's alien yet familiar, real yet mystical, natural though often awkward to come by or express. It fits the description of self, the situation of attempting to look within to see who's looking, hence considering it identity-revealing rather than solely a feeling.

I don't expect; I accept and decide. That's freedom to me, to my lovers. You do you, whatever that may be, as I do the same. And if that means you walk my heart only to leave me one morning, well, thank you for the dance.

We could also consider love as a channel transferring information across time, dimensions, space and the universe. For example, if my mother were to leave this realm, I know I would still be able to feel her love flowing throughout my being, communicating with my soul, and that's not a matter of my mind attempting to source her presence from memories to handle grief, pulling together fragmented parts of our history for comfort. Once again, that's dumbing down the human experience by ironically presenting a sophisticated scientific model of reality. Instead, I philosophise my mother's energy persists within my being, communicating, guiding, and loving, not as a spirit or ghost but intrinsically as myself. After all, her body, her nature, created my form. I am of her and my father, and so forth, back until we reach Mother Nature. Love, it seems, is an antenna. If we tune into ourselves, we understand it. We realise it's not something to lose or gain but channel. Knowing this, you can cultivate self-love by directly interacting with the source through meditative practices. Consequently, sensitive events such as losing a loved one, be it from death or rejection, aren't as heavy on the heart because you understand you haven't lost anything, for you never had anything more than what is already flowing throughout your entirety, which is everything. That amplifies love and influences a playful attitude when feeling the force. Rather than stress about finding it or holding on to it, you stand, spread your arms, and surf the wave, knowing there's an ocean of love within you, ready to catch your fall.

Falling out of love, if we should even call it that, really isn't that bad if your perception involves gratitude; if you approach the experience feeling thankful that you had the opportunity to meet another soul like yourself during your brief moment under the sun. To think, "wow, how wonderful I met another person so profoundly." The contrary response involves attachment, 'mine,' an investment of identity within a relationship that'll inevitably end, causing immense grief from a feeling of rejection, a loss of self. I have experienced this many times. I couldn't handle rejection. Love sucked. However, after delving into philosophy, unlearning, and practising this newfound understanding, I experience relationships differently, more raw, honest, accepting, and I must say, what magnificence. The romance is genuine, the relationship real, the departure - bittersweet. The interactions are authentic, so the sex is orgasmic, for no clothing is left on the soul.

Rejection is a form of guidance so long as self-worth is internally sourced and not externally identified. Otherwise, irrational emotions will overwhelm you as your psyche scrambles to find reassurance, potentially leading to frantic immature decisions.

Sex is more than a reproductive activity. That's obvious with the eccentric cultures curiously exploring the intimate engagement. Like love, sex is transcending. It destroys barriers. It reforms one's state of mind, altering reality from an egocentric venture into a unified experience. It's like communicating without speaking or knowing without thinking. However, if approached as a process with an objective, it becomes tasteless, like eating strictly to attain nutrients. When those involved aren't wholly engaged, they situate themselves in an awkward position, stuck inside their minds as their connection is thought-based and disconnected from feeling, for the ego is still the primary viewpoint, disrupting the moment. Soulful sex is playful, expressive and communicative. There's no intent but to touch one another, truly, to interact as cheeky monkeys having fun with the physical manifestation of their energy by surrendering themselves to the moment, in which they become the climax.

Sex, for me, has transcended into an ethereal bonding through strength and surrender, giving and receiving. It's become a space of consciously feeling another's existence, from energy to soul, mind to body, in and out, stripping the universe down to its source. It's meaningful and passionate, a soulfully insightful practice.

Love and sex provide insight into our mystery. They are not merely biological phenomena evolved for survival. They're spiritually informative, revealing, exposing a metaphysical face that is much more ours than mine. To know love is to be it; to be it is to live courageously, vulnerable, naked, as you turn yourself inside out. It's empowering as you shift away from strictly living within the confinements of ego and instead undergo the human experience predominantly from a perspective of surrender. That is to unify your consciousness with the collective happening, meaning you realise yourself to be out there, everywhere, and not within your head as a mere thought. Hence, you exude love, for what is more sensible than loving oneself?

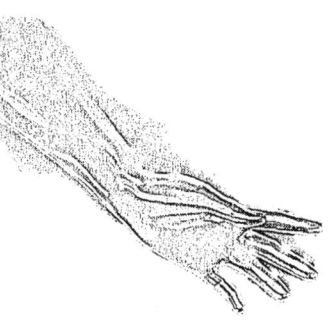

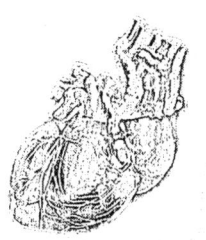

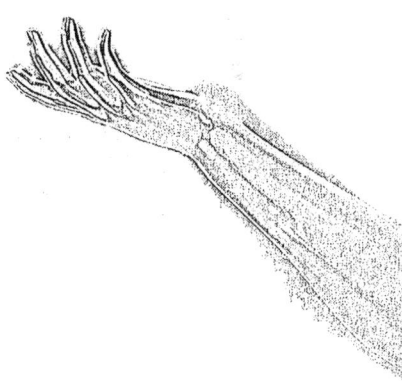

You want love, you want it so badly, but there's no one around. You want your body touched, your soul kissed, your heart held in the palm of another. You want your whole universe to expand with dopamine and nothing else. You want them to find you, to save you, to bring you everything and anything. You want to share the late nights, the sunrises, the brief time you have left. You want to see what happens when a human meets another human beyond this realm of ordinary interaction. You want one day of ecstasy before you die, one day of orgasmic sex, love and soulful engagements. You want to annihilate your existence within their eyes; you want to find yourself within their eyes. You want to watch the world end as you hold hands and wildly dance in your living room, listening to music while you go mad with laughter, screaming at the strangeness of life. You want to extract the mystery poetically by detailing their presence linguistically and then read it to them. You want to grow old with a lover and then fall into a black hole together, only to awake within another universe and start all over. You want all of this, don't you?

I understand you're attracted to them and wish they'd see you, feel you, but this moment that you have, that you are, isn't worth sacrificing to acquire their attention. If there's anything between you both, particularly love, it will happen; they will gravitate toward you. But trying to force this, especially at the expense of your immediate experience, is to go against the universe. That will only cause you pain.

There's no better way to destroy oneself than to fall in love.

The tragedy of modern romance is that a self-aware individual will struggle to find love in a society and culture that devalues conscious interaction.

I think I married a witch in my previous life because I am haunted by a powerful love not of this world.

Be it from my foolery or charm, causing a woman I love to laugh feels innately meaningful.

People are awkward with love, and it's no coincidence. We're an insecure society sourcing identity from an anti-human culture. We feel more comfortable arguing economics and politics than intimately dancing with one another because we fear what we are by nature. And there lies our misery.

My love is rare; my lover, rarer.

Presence is necessary for connection. You must be vulnerable, naked, here, in all your humanness. For how else can you be touched? Felt? Loved?

Let go of your lover. Take a step back. Remove the cultured glasses, see them more clearly, less polluted with your insecurities manifested linguistically and interactively. Recognise their individuality and independence. Acknowledge them before you as another wonder of the universe, a freak of nature that you're just thankful to have had the opportunity to encounter.

Comedy is the forgotten sibling of poetry. If you love a woman,
write her a joke.

If your lover cannot freely speak their truth, be as they are, then no love can be felt, for there's no one there to feel, for no one's themselves. To demand loyalty is to lack trust. It states, "I am fragile, so devote yourself to me, tell me you're mine. Give me a sense of security because I fear change. I fear the truth. I fear to feel, for above all, I fear myself."

Every now and then, someone from another world enters our universe and expands it with love.

Tell me, what is sense to love? What is reason, logic or reality to this ethereal experience where creatures dimensionally transcend through the portals of each other's soul? I am not in love, though I have been - so I guess I still am - but when I think of those who presented what I would describe as a surreal force engulfing my entirety, I'm speechless. Extraordinary. I don't fear love or envy those who feel it, so I won't trivialise something clearly unearthly by referring to scientific observation, pretending it's merely chemical related. It's alien yet familiar. Real but mystical. It's a reminder of what we are behind this veil, and to lift it through conscious engagement with oneself or another is to witness the ineffable.

To say I'm yours and claim you as mine would be an awful lie.

I'm a basic man. I'm easily charmed by an honest woman.

So much suffering, chaos and destruction within and without, yet I have such a strong, innate desire to love.

We want to feel and be felt, but we're afraid to be vulnerable, so our words lack meaning, our space lacks presence, our energy misinforms what is true, and so we're left untouched, unloved and unknown.

/MΛIND/

Here we are, fleshly, bodily, tangible - a biological concoction of god knows what. Although, what else is here that concerns a tremendous amount of our being yet supposedly unseen is our mind; the multidimensional, transformative alien-like matrix arguably hosting an entire universe worth of possibility.

The location of the mind feels as though it's somewhere within, such as the brain, but as seen, it predominantly resides externally, exposed throughout the world in the form of art, speech, movement, decisions, interactions, designs, constructs, etcetera. The mind is infinite, leaking from our finite matter, and I think it's an underlying substance of the universe fragmented and engulfed by form. We've embodied whatever this intelligent field is and tangibly taken hostage a fraction of this enigmatic exotic property that provides the ability to imagine, think, and create - which is what I believe the universe to be doing. It's a dream dreaming dreamers who, in turn, dream. Concerning this thought, humans innately biologically host a relatively large chunk of this transcending cosmic feature. As a result, our minds are extensive compared to other known creatures. We're big dreamers, artists, and thinkers. Perhaps how is due to coercing Mother Nature through natural habitual practices such as routinely digesting psychedelics to influence evolutionary change in how big of a slice we mindfully embody throughout each new generation.

So long as there are artists, thinkers, dreamers, and lovers - there is hope.

When I consider the mind, which is the mind's hallucinated character 'ego,' operating mind, I intuitively envision an infinite space impregnated by consciousness and somehow withheld to a certain extent by the material realm in which we wander. We are a balance of mind, body (or energy depending on the perspective,) and consciousness momentarily happening. It's a love triangle. Although, eventually, something will give way, usually the body, leading to what is meant by death and what happens to our means of existence is anyone's guess. However, if there's anything to go off what I'm philosophically presenting here with 'the mind,' perhaps dying is each intrinsic component returning to their respective wombs. Our energy vibrates an indigenous frequency awaiting novel interaction in the material plane; our mind returns to the exotic intelligent field of dreams; our awareness recedes like a wave to the collective consciousness. I suggest this for when I specifically philosophise the mind, particularly psychological aspects, I observe a longing for annihilation as though my mind is bashing against the temporal walls of my body. I realise I often urge to disappear - to fragment until I'm void. It's not a depressive mood nor of any concern. Instead, I believe it to be hereditary; I've inherited it from the universe, for I think that's precisely a part of its dream. Because by becoming nothing or breaking off into little bits, I can become whole again. These words are fragments of me, the ichor of my mind and soul dripping into vision through symbols for a textual appearance. But if I did not do this or occasionally feel the desire to disappear, leak myself out of the physical, my experience of existence would be incomplete. I could never be whole. Hence, I wisely choose the best method - art. Therefore, if you're ever in this state of mind, don't fight it or think of it to be negative. Let yourself dissolve through forms of art to flourish and grow.

The egoless state is perfection. This moment is everything. Surrendering to the universe is completion. But I must state that my mind is somewhat of a universe itself, and although I am cognitively restricted, I intellectually feel infinite, rich with ancient knowledge awaiting my plundering through introspection.

In all its complexity and intricacy, the depth of the mind can feel like a burden to consciously handle; thus, our efforts to mentally intoxicate ourselves with ideas, drugs, and reality itself. Many abhor their mind, preferring to avoid direct interaction through mindful practices, such as meditation, and even going as far as subconsciously projecting internal security mechanisms to deter self-reflection. For example, fearing silent darkness and believing in negative entities such as demonic spirits is a subconscious attempt to prevent mindfulness. The psyche projects these ghostly distractions to discourage conscious apprehension of a momentous psychological revelation. That the only monster under the bed, inside your head, within your immediate space, is the part of you that you refuse to acknowledge.

We've scientifically presented a study to lessen the conundrum of existing with such an exotic mental property, which is psychology, although psychology sometimes overcomplicates problems and detours one toward a solution. Indeed, the study is paramount for revealing and healing problematic psychological matters, but some mental relief or stability is achievable by simply getting over yourself. Relax, go for a walk, breathe, laugh, cry, dance, and listen to music. Let yourself go. Ironically, partially, psychology as a practice integrated within modern society has influenced the birth of a culture looking for problems. It's becoming normal to have something wrong with you, almost as if it's fashionable.

I was once suicidal. I had severe body issues, social anxiety, and agoraphobia. I periodically took medication; I was a regular on the ol' detour. It wasn't until I began figuring myself out in solitude that I realised nothing was wrong. Sure, there were negative aspects to change to benefit my health and those around me, some deeply rooted in the unconscious, but I didn't require the terminology or books to understand, nor did I need an individual just as disturbing as me charging over a hundred dollars for a diagnosis. All that was necessary for some mental relief was for me to get over myself.

I have sung and danced my way out of some dark times. Literally.

We are whatever we say we are, as the world is whatever we imagine it to be. The mind creates reality, and reality influences the mind. Imagination is the link between both and potentially the museum of the universe. What is now real once lay dormant in the unreal. Therefore, note the power of the mind. It is capable of transcending what is impossible and making it possible. If you find yourself in an unfavourable position, against all odds, you possess this mental property capable of overcoming the situation. All it takes is a confrontation with oneself. To go within consciously, meditate and communicate with self. If we avoid this, which is to live 'mindlessly' by consciously or unconsciously submitting to institutions and ideologies that think for us, we lose such boundless power.

There is, in my opinion, an agenda against the mind. I rationalise this based on the economic and education system and its nature of breeding humans into roles that involve tiresome labour but no mental stimulation. Businesses capitalise on selling addictive goods at the expense of the customer's health, psychological or physical. School subjects lack human engagement; there's no concern for spirit, energy or inner self. Money is symbolised as the purpose of life, imprinted into the subconscious of many people as something truly significant. Evidently, support for expanding the human mind is not in the best interest of the institutions leading human civilisation. People lack the network or space which motivates or encourages conscious expansion and, therefore, self-knowledge through mindfulness. They instead seep into ideology and consumerism for fulfilment and direction. They become as much a product as the products they consume, eaten alive by the very system they feed.

Hence, I hold much suspicion toward those overlooking the direction in which we progress as a civilisation, such as government, for I can only conclude the overall approach to education is purposefully baleful relative to developing healthy minded societal members. Understandably, as I mentioned previously, referencing economic collapse, variables are at play; it is a complex situation to cultivate a sustainable environment while factoring numerous humans and the egoic luggage they harbour. Yet, we work together globally, and that is remarkable. But how we accomplish this is primarily through anti-human concepts that create counterfeit connections, such as money, and so this world of unity hangs on an illusion, ready to dismantle and reveal the consequences of minds that neglected mindfulness.

If an unprecedented event rattles the mind of a human who neglected self-examination, the inner animal's cage breaks, the ego flees, and the world is mauled.

For you see, suppose you fetishise world domination for whatever reason. Perhaps you righteously believe you know what's best for humanity, and let's say that's the attitude and agenda of the elite. Well, war isn't the way. Force is amateur. Instead, manipulate the thought process of the intended through mind tunnelling. Control how they interact with information by constructing reference points within their cognition. Slowly, linguistically dig your way into their psyche, preferably while they're young, and begin laying the ideological framework through efficient, reputable institutions such as culture, science, and religion. After some time, you won't have to invest in regular maintenance of these tunnels, as the targets will egotistically manifest a character who'll freely work to preserve the infrastructure. They'll reinforce the implanted perspectives as their truth and defend it with their lives while fundamentally identifying themselves as this character. Brilliantly too, they'll act as salesmen selling your infrastructure throughout their social network. It's free marketing and labour. Don't restrict independent thinking either; that's an unprofessional move. Instead, provide just enough freedom to delude one into believing their thoughts are free of external influence to reduce potential suspicion and, consequently, introspection. Otherwise, they'll discover the construction through self-awareness. However, if all runs smoothly, no matter their perspective, all information will transport through the tunnels you constructed. Soon enough, the desired reality will be projected by the intended, and with enough minds, dominate the collective consciousness. As a result, attainment of world domination.

Whether this is happening or not cannot factually be said. However, our minds are mistreated. We are exposed to information by various channels that feed rather than offer. Therefore, we ought to be self-aware of our thoughts. Understand what it is that you think and why. Utilise your inteligence. Retake your universe. Traverse your mind through mindfulness. Otherwise, you risk giving up an invaluable tool that influences your reality - the sails to your mortal voyage.

Suicide is not unnatural; everyone considers it whether they realise it or not - for no animal this biologically primitive yet intellectually godly remains mentally stable without some form of spiritual practice easing the intensity of consciousness. Therefore, we all make a choice. You either familiarise yourself with silence or solely depend on distractions to prevent you from killing yourself. Because underlying our motives to consume or invent is an intent to distract the mind from focusing on the void expanding within that reminds us nothing lasts, nothing matters, and nothingness will soon devour us whole.

I fear consumerist culture is spreading outside of the material and leaking into the realm of the intellect. I fear we're no longer investing ourselves in the information we attain; that we're instead preferring to buy what others or groups of people such as governments have to sell. We're consuming ideas, facts, beliefs, thoughts - but the average individual isn't producing them. We cannot allow ourselves to strictly become customers of knowledge, buying what we cannot be bothered to understand for ourselves. We cannot starve the intellect because if we do, businesses will capitalise on profiting from intellectual commodities, and as the customer base grows, these non-tangible goods will take little to no effort to make. We'll believe the most absurd truths. We'll normalise and accept foolishness, which will stupefy the general population.

Your mind is invaluable. It's the most exotic, one-of-a-kind supernatural treasure in the known universe. To recklessly trade such a profound alien property for an ideology or shallow pursuit like money is incredibly unwise. Use your mind; dream, dream and dream some more. Consciously explore its depths; extract and translate remnants of the mystery. Perceptively push the boundaries of this realm. Shake hands with the source. Create art, for God's sake.

To leave the wonders of my mind unexplored would be a shame, considering it contains the vastness of a universe.

Social media is a window to a psych ward.

People keep door-knocking my mind trying to sell me a better version of myself. What a scam.

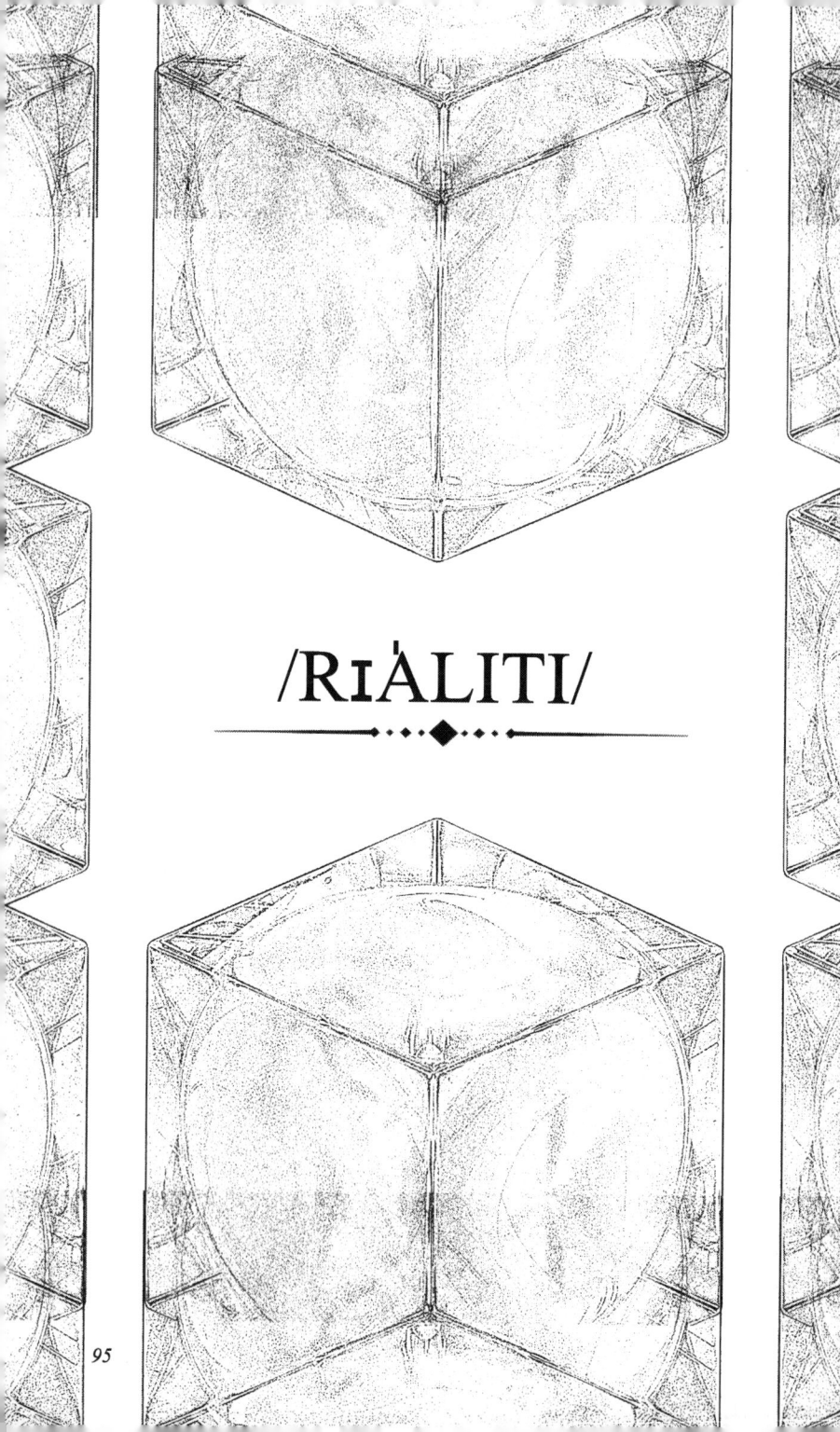

/Rɪ'ALITI/

/RIÀLITI/

When I question what is real, I intend to assimilate a definitive answer to what's genuinely here. Something tangible, perpetual, unaffected by the perception or awareness of another. Unfortunately, however, realising such a 'thing' is challenging. As discussed earlier, physicality is deceptive, and it's near impossible to confirm what's before us isn't a hallucination, considering how chemically overwhelmed we are by the complexity of the weird cosmic ingredients constituting our biological happening. Moreover, stating I am real is questionable, for the 'I' referred to is channelled through language by the tunnel of ego. Consciousness seems most reliable. However, consciousness is difficult to explain, for we can't say what it isn't or pinpoint its location, yet it's everywhere. It's elusive. For example, the only difference between this world and when I'm dreaming is where I consciously am. I cannot wholly remember my dream, just as when I'm dreaming - I cannot remember this world. And if I happen to remember, I'm pulled back here, like when I become unconscious, I go elsewhere. So it seems the validity of reality and our existence is quite fragile. And if we cannot prove ourselves to be legitimate, how can we define what is?

Everyone's schizophrenic, hallucinating a reality, inventing characters, creating Gods, believing truths, hearing a voice, and searching for self. We're inside our mind, in the corner of ego, walking into a wall of thoughts, talking to ourselves. We're insane, a bunch of atoms, particles, chemicals, matter, stuff mushed together, high on its essence, trying to make sense of the nonsensical.

To define the limits of reality is arrogant and historically impulsive. Truth varies with each moment that passes, even if it's only slightly. Still, people offer cognitive tools and resort to external sources such as science to present a solid, objective outline of what's true. Science, however, is to reality what grammar is to language. It offers an effective means of translating, of communicating this happening for collective understanding, but it doesn't explain anything. Immediately one may argue we've explained how certain things work and benefited as a result but have we, really? Answers always birth more questions; technological advancements have only revealed more of our ignorance. Science is adding punctuation to the message, but that's as far as it goes. We have no solid basis of reasoning, for what are we referring to when cementing our stance? Look around you; logically speaking, existence is illogical.

Everything about us defies all sensible reasoning, and deep down, we know this - we know we're inexplainable, unknown, which scares us, so we subconsciously alter our rationale toward fantasy and reason from a fictitious world where we can make sense of ourselves with false security. We tell stories - reality - and if we don't, we're confronted by the void that begets our whole and inundated by paradoxes. Ironically then, with this perspective, truth is of fiction, sense from nonsense, real from unreal, because the world is a story we imagine to experience, along with the character we identify as I, and the moment we attempt to look beyond that, we cease altogether. Before you think this is all ludicrous, consider what is real was once unreal, such as yourself, for where exactly have you been for the past thirteen billion years of the observable universe? Some years ago, you never existed. Now, here you are. The same goes for our arts, crafts and inventions. We litter this realm with remenants extracted from the unknown. So when we investigate what is real, we cannot ignore what we believe isn't, for eventually, it becomes real. Everything here today was either someplace else or nowhere. If nowhere, then perhaps nothing is what's real. Nothingness is self-sustaining, perpetual, and unaffected by anything external. Everything is more like a hallucination arising from the void. But this is a significant contradiction, downright mind-bending and wild as we conclude what is non-existent is real, and what exists is unreal; that everything comes from nothing.

No one perceives the same universe. In that sense, we're living in a multi-verse. What is true to you isn't necessarily true to me. The same goes for what is real.

Another candidate for identifying what's real is change. Change encapsulates all. It's undying, timeless, inevitable, unavoidable, and tangible throughout the physical realm - a prerequisite of the universe. You are a subject of change, as are truth and fantasy. It's happening naturally, and no matter the situation, it will persist.

Change reveals reality. It outlines what is experienced by the perceiver. To resist change is to go against the nature of your existence, as change is what sets in motion your venture, for through light and dark, loss and gain, joy and pain, sun and rain - you happen. Hence the philosophy of surrender. By giving into change, we are gifted growth. However, that does not mean giving up; giving up is stagnation, refusing to accept reality, weighing heavily with negative energy, retreating from living, thus preventing transformation. Giving in is to flow with change, to adjust without attachment - a process of metamorphosis. You can fight with all your might and still host a fundamental philosophy of surrender because you understand and accept change will pursue. That helps with areas of life that are emotionally challenging to deal with, such as breakups or rejection as you accept the circumstances and persevere.

It is unwise to oppose change. Nothing lasts perhaps besides love. Even our most refined scientific understandings eventually give way, yet billions of humans continue to source absolute truth in what they deem unwavering sources of information. They seek permanence and deliverance from the *unknown* via inarguable truths such as an almighty creator - God.

What's real is change. Go back millions of years, and you have colossal creatures roaming a young Earth. Before that, a cloud of dust and gas. Fast-forward to now, and you have upright, walking, talking primates traversing virtual reality and documenting the cosmos.

Say, through every word, belief, or fact, we add a layer of clothing to our body, ironically distorting ourselves in an attempt to define and identify ourselves. Hence, reality. However, someone mentions these layers are fundamentally misleading, no matter how convincing the clothing seems. As a result, they add a layer of clothing, as that's a belief. Although this seems contradictory, it strengthens in its demise, for whether the layer of clothing is taken off or left on, the philosophical proposition remains sound. It's proven correct in its undoing. That is the basis of my philosophical perspective regarding reality.

So much certainty for a creature drugged by its anatomy.

Reality is a major misunderstanding.

I cannot overlook our bizarre predicament. That's why I love philosophy. I'm like a child pulling on 'God's beard.' I'm face-to-face with the unknown, staring, watching, questioning, laughing, listening and experiencing. I'm curious. What the hell is this? Seriously?

Whatever you think to be true, debate it, and think again.

Being a realist means you realise how unreal this all is, and that it's changeable. You don't supposedly go from nothingness to universe, to galaxies, to planets, to organic life, to humans, to running stock markets and attending speed dating sessions like it's a daily checklist. "This is how it is" isn't how it is at all; this is what we've made it to be, from the politics to the economic system, society and culture. We created the world.

So I hang with the spiritual and eccentric as a hardcore sceptic predominantly favouring intellect to cognise this experience because I cannot stand the mentality of most rationalists. Ironically, they're the most irrational people claiming to be rational by strictly keeping their hands inside the boat while they sail a dream.

I'm a writer who thinks primarily through images; a fool who intellectualises through introspection and empathy; a realist who realises this realm's unrealness.

/GØD/

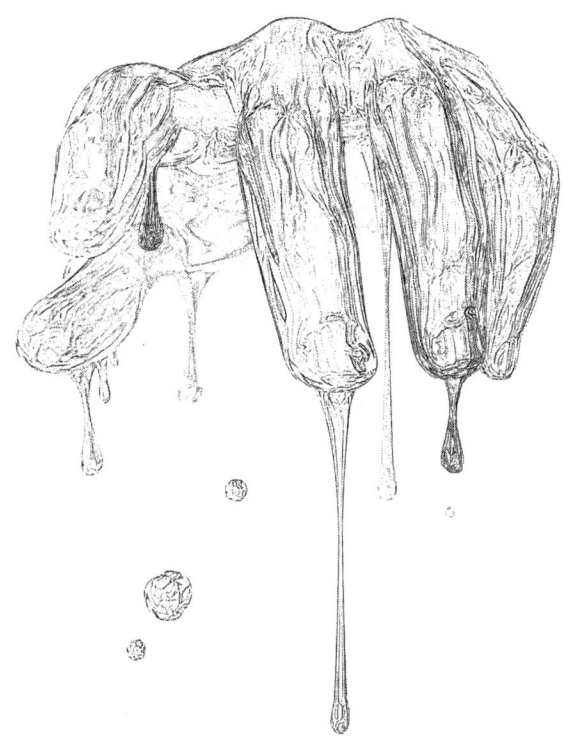

In essence, according to the many prevalent religions, a creator termed 'God' constructed the universe. 'He' is faithfully real within the minds of many, notably those who believe the validity of the doctrines telling the existence of an omnipotent creator. Whether you believe in God or not, it doesn't matter, for my perspective is harmless. So, do note there is no biased opinion favouring an argumentive position. I am neither religious nor atheist. I do not care what is ultimately true, only that I do not stray from such revelation by avoiding deep contemplation or self-examination because I admit I know nothing. To the best of my intelligence and consciousness, what little I have, I will philosophise God.

God, as a creator, is no foolish concept. After all, from our realm, what we can observe, creation takes place. Everywhere we look, numerous events implicate novel forms emerging throughout the domain of activity we call life. Art is a perfect example, as was your birth. Therefore, considering the universe as a matter of creation, particularly from an overseeing source, is reasonable. If anything, strictly from human perception, it is more sound to believe in God than to settle with the Big Bang theory as an explanation. The Big Bang theory suggests the sudden emergence of the cosmos from a single point, for no attributed purpose, without meaning. Of all possibilities, that is least relevant to human understanding, for there is no noun initiating the verb. However, is it arrogant to assume the universe should make sense according to how we rationalise existence, especially from a matter of language?

As you look around you, observing the external, the people walking by, the clouds passing above, the birds flying about - make note you experience as much as your form permits. You are physically limited to a three-dimensional construct, though mindfully partially fleeing into a fourth via the gateway of the imagination and time through memory. Considering this situation, we must factor in the grandiose unknown dwarfing our every apparent truth or belief, for what may make sense here might be untrue, trivial or irrelevant from a higher dimensional perspective. We can, of course, acknowledge this with the various species surrounding us who are oblivious to celestial activity governing their planet, let alone the fact they're on what we term a 'planet.' It is also continually recognised with each novel truth that overwrites a previous one, such as the scientific discoveries throughout history. We alter reality daily. The basic notion then of knowing God contradicts the evolution of humankind's cognition. Our Gods cannot keep up with our growth.

If hypothetically, I dematerialised, consciously transcended, persisting energetically, only to rematerialise as something alien from a higher dimension, I doubt God survives, at least not the God known to man, which refutes religion.

When my religious friends speak to me of God, describing this ineffable source flowing throughout the spectrum of their entirety, they say, "He's undeniable, for denial would be a rejection of self. In prayer, his voice is felt, not heard. In life, his guidance is everywhere, morally unearthed. We are his children, thoroughly loved and cherished. God may be a concept, but his presence is not."

Although, in this, I find it challenging to legitimise God objectively, and consequently, understand the notion to be self-projected, for I fundamentally cannot differentiate up from down, in from out, life from death, self from other, good from bad, and so forth, for they all imply one another. Listening to my friends detail him and express what they believe to be accurate, their description offers nothing which opposed this viewpoint, enlightening a new perspective, which indicated, in my opinion, their belief to be psychologically founded on the back of sincere spiritual reflection. To connect with their God, they project what is communicated within, externalising an inner divine experience with self by identifying it as an encounter with God. What they undergo, say through prayer, is real, powerful, though misconstrued by ego, as they channel the interaction through that reference point. Aside from cultural conditioning, I can only assume a plausible explanation for why they consciously and linguistically redirect their divinity through an external identity is due to severe self-doubt, which entails dependency and potentially a fear of leaving the nest. When they say they believe in God, what is meant is they do not think such a powerful presence could be their own.

Of course, this does not disprove God - it only offers a possibility of explaining the psychology of numerous religious individuals and their beliefs. God supersedes parents. If one has an attachment complexity, they may be more inclined to convince themselves of a God hosting the desired attributes to be true for the continuation of their comfort. The same goes for someone without a father figure or who holds a negative relationship with their elders. God, an overseeing parent who loves you, offers an opportunity to fill that void. We have, as a species, for thousands of years told stories to get us through the night, the unknown, and the existence of this divine creator may very well be such a fantastical story for psychological motives. After all, do we not feel alone? Cheeky monkeys consciously comprehending what perhaps they were not ready to discover? As curious children of the cosmos, we've prematurely snuck a look under the dress of the universe, and we look to the concept of God as we did to our parents for comfort in understanding. Thus the invention of religion.

Religion and God are two separate matters. At least that's what they are today. God concerns God. Religion, however, is controlling, debilitating, and misleading. Historically, it's a destructive system claiming the foundation of man's morality by implanting fallacious truths that override one's sense of empathy and conscious reasoning by rerouting contact with self through some ideology. It attempts to define reality in conservatism, which is contradictory, for all truth is momentary. It values symbols over interaction, hierarchy over a connection, faith over scepticism - it distorts the proposition of a universal creator into a manifestation of ego. The Gods identified through religion reveal more about man's psyche than the source of a creator. That's important for both believers and non-believers to comprehend. When you entertain the possibility of our origin as divine design, differentiate what's presented by religion and the basic philosophical proposition of a creator. Philosophise the idea yourself. Otherwise, your relationship with God - your image of God - isn't between you and God but between you and another's idea of God.

Another factor of religion to examine is religious faith. Faith is highly unreasonable as a basis for defining truth. For example, say you faithfully believed in a divine creator, you know what is factual and moral according to this Supreme Being. However, you were opposed by another who shared the same rationale for uncovering truth. They know God demands child sacrifice every fortnight but you know he doesn't. Yet, you and this individual feel you are correct from head to toe, and toe to soul. Paradoxically, the medium of communicating God is shared, though the message is drastically different. That is the fragility of religious faith and the injudicious implication of determining God by such means.

Listen, let's hypothetically actualise a creator. There 'it' is, in the flesh. And we say, "Wow, it's God. God turns around. "Who the hell is that?"

To argue in favour of God's existence, I think we should question how such concepts exist. Where do ideas come from? We haven't the slightest clue aside from a simplistic explanation of combining influences from direct experiences of reality and dreaming, which trigger creative thought. However, that doesn't reveal much at all. What is the imagination? Could it be because we can conceive a universal creator, it actually exists somewhere? Of course, an immediate contradiction would arise from recognising ideas that cancel each other out. Nevertheless, the proposition still stands, and I don't think it is wise to dismiss the possibility of a divine creator or wholly devote oneself to believing one exists. And if death is one's reason for belief, as they feel the unknown is too daunting, than the foundation of the belief is insincere, and the perspective towards death is misconstrued, for fearing death is fearing birth.

What a bore it'd be to be someone who believes they know everything.

Perhaps behind my logic and reasoning toward doubting the concept of God, particularly the Christian God as I was raised Christian, is that I refuse to accept it was not my mother who weaved her magic to form my being. I owe my existence to her divine ability, and I cannot - be it stupidity or stubbornness - subscribe to any notion which disempowers her in favour of faith in an omnipotent, masculine figure. I cannot support any religious doctrine where a belief founded by men attempts to steal the miraculous nature which rightfully and solely belongs to women. I think this psychologically, in part, influences my appreciation of scientific theories of creation such as Darwinism, for it's a return to Mother Nature, the feminine, for answers regarding our existence.

I have had the privilege of doubting God.

If a supernatural overlord is indeed judging our every move, ready to erase our species upon dissatisfaction, surely it's our artists, particularly our comedians and musicians buying us some time.

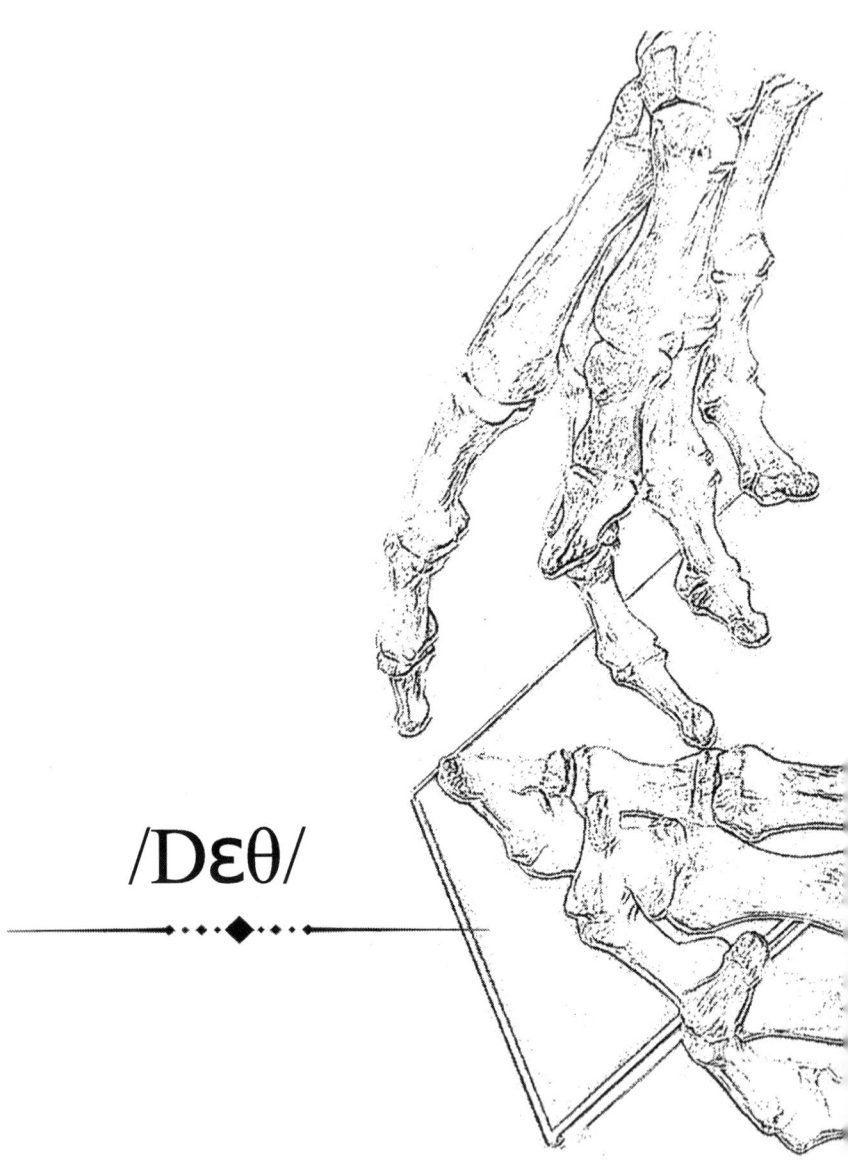

/Dɛθ/

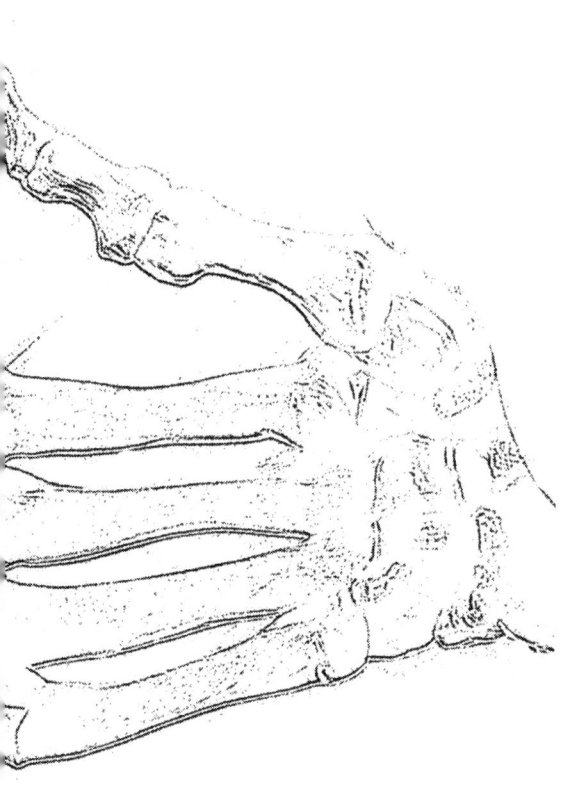

Death is confusing. To be aware of it is daunting. The matter exposes a state contrary to what we're accustomed to experiencing. From an everyday perspective, life is brimful, thrilling, and expressive. Death, however, is empty, still, dull. It makes no sense. An organism arises overloaded with activity, only to suddenly vanish as if they were never here. Depending on the depth, to share a relationship with another, be them human or non-human, and lose that connection to death is like switching the stars off within the universe and the light within your heart. It all goes dark. I remember struggling to comprehend my cousin's passing as a kid. She was a couple of years older than me, thirteen, and I vividly recall sitting before her casket in the church, waiting for her to stand up and announce herself alive. It was the first time I consciously assimilated death, and I'm virtually just as puzzled.

Death is instrumental to life. It defines the living, sculpting the organically animate. Your formation within your mother's womb involved plenty of death. It was the momentum of your metamorphosis and still is today. Right now, plenty about you is dying, especially if you're past your twenties, and all around you as well, the fungi, fauna and flora are perishing. Death is ubiquitous yet mysterious. Without it, life as we know it wouldn't be organically possible regarding the necessary changes that rejuvenate the physical environment, be it your body or surroundings or even the non-physical, with thoughts, relationships, knowledge and wisdom. So, why, generally speaking, do we fear death? Is it our attachment to momentary normality? Or anxiety toward the suffering involved with dying? Or fear of what's next, if anything? I think it's that and more, though I believe we can change our attitude and be more accepting of death, which will, in return, improve our experience of life. To do that, we must reconsider how we view what it means to be alive. Part of that is comprehending what's involved with our entirety, such as space and silence.

Space and silence host attributes similar to death, as they are the inactive essentials bearing the platform for life. Curiously, just like death, we dismiss them as foreign, yet both are as intrinsic to our being as matter and sound. Space dominates the external, yet so too are we more space than anything else. Therefore, to acknowledge ourselves wholly, we must be aware of this, to see ourselves within the void and the void within us. As a result, we can assimilate a novel perspective toward death, as death is an expression of space and silence. You embody these two fundamental forces. I feel, based on this, that my loved ones who have parted this realm are right here with me, in stillness, in nothingness, internally and externally, between the stars. Through meditation, self-reflection, and stillness, I can sense their presence, not as an individual character or ego, but as the underlying origin of all life.

Existing within silence is a part of me, and long after I'm dead, in that silence I will live.

Let's perceive death from another angle, and regard the cessation of the body and mind. We know it's coming. You and I are going to change drastically until an eventual stop. Hypothetically, for argument's sake, consider dying in your sleep, perhaps from old age complications. If we envision or observe this scenario, the state is frightening, though oddly peaceful. The energy permitting our form slows, our cellular activity stops, and our bodies begin to decay. The state of consciousness is unknown, as no one knows precisely how consciousness works. That implies your passing from this realm may involve 'conscious recession.' Right now, as a three-dimensional organism, you operate with a particular state of awareness founded by your senses. That awareness is arguably fundamentally you. What's in question is the circumstances of stripping back an organism of its biological 'antennas' that channel consciousness. For example, if you lose sight, your conscious experience alters. As goes for your other senses. So, when you're deemed clinically dead, are you experiencing a form of awareness enabled by the circumstances of your body? Perhaps consciously, we recede until we physically fragment into nothingness, nirvana, the underlying state of all. From there, you're the source.

On the other hand, consciousness may be singular though infinite. It may be neither here nor there but elsewhere, unlocatable, undefinable. As such, you may be somewhat of an independent universe, hosting past lives and living eternally as an immortal force periodically materialising throughout this field of activity. If that's the situation, then the afterlife is life. You continue, forever, as energy changing form. It may be so that now you appear as a human, tomorrow an alien. And all it takes is enough conscious disconnection from the matter hosting you currently. We understand this line of thinking as reincarnation.

Another possibility of entertaining an afterlife is questioning the evolution and death of the mind. If the mind, as mentioned earlier, is an intrinsic property of the universe, somewhat withheld by the body, perhaps it's relinquished come death, and after passing, one's conscious experience becomes strictly mind-related. Death is a gateway into the realm of dreams, though as the dreamer, one is awake and in control, for they are no longer tangible. The only arguably perplexing view toward this suggestion is considering non-human organisms who seemingly host shallow minds, such as bacteria or insects.

But who knows? Or better yet, what ego can know? Deep down, some may feel they know, apparent in meditative states of enlightenment or prayer, but it's impossible to translate the revelation egoically. That is why I doubt ego survives death, continuing in the afterlife as many religious beliefs suggest. I see that as least plausible because the ego is a total fabrication misconstruing identity. To think spirits go about eternity with their name, nationality, race, and political agendas, debating the best generation of music as though energy stores such trivial information is humourous. I doubt that. And don't be fooled by your current human perception to find another life unfavourable. That's biased thinking relative to your current manifestation.

I look at you and think, ha, there I am, pulling a different face. Do you not feel the same? Do you not feel that we, along with everything, are instruments of the same song? It's all going to wash over us come death.

The number of dead beings tremendously outweighs the living. I think that's important to reflect on. For billions of years ~ most likely far longer relative to possible organic extraterrestrial lifeforms in the universe ~ creatures have come and gone. Right now, you probably feel yourself to be singular, meaningful, living a story in which you're the protagonist. To a degree, this is true, in your window to the universe. But ultimately, you're another passenger passing by, just like the numerous organisms that have come and gone. You're insignificant, which can lead to a lack of enthusiasm for life, for why do anything if everything you do ultimately means nothing? It's kind of funny that your life has no real impact. It may play a part in the butterfly effect, influencing events greater than your happening, but it doesn't mean anything. Aside from your family and friends' perspective, when you die, it'll be as if you were never here. Even if you're well known or continuously achieve remarkable feats, it doesn't matter because this whole planet is going up in flames - all of it. Soon, it'll just be space. And that begs the question, what of everything? What is the point of existence? Yes, perhaps we're too ignorant to realise our significance, but it doesn't look promising from what we can see. Therefore, be it individually or collectively, our lives are seemingly meaningless; unless we redefine what we mean by meaning.

I think we're cultured to identify significance through productivity and progression. If these are missing, we believe whatever we're doing to be of no importance. If one philosophically entertains death, they realise productivity and advancement are pointless, which can be discouraging, especially for artists. However, I'd like to provide an alternative understanding of discerning meaning: base it on play. Consider love, for I find it rich with meaning. When I love someone, I don't expect it to be productive. I don't think it is progressive either. Love, to me, is playful - that's what it means. It doesn't matter what it becomes or the fact it'll end; the purpose is in the joy of intimately grooving with someone. It's a dance, and like dancing, you don't work your way to the end of the song - you let yourself go and have fun while you feel the music.

It's our privilege as humans. We have this 'secret' little paradise out here in space - it's almost like a getaway from all the chaos occurring throughout the cosmos - and we're engaged in a vibrating play of energy. So, therefore, value meaning in play, and the purpose of play is to involve oneself in mystery. Death, therefore, isn't a worry. It's a change in dance to the same song called life.

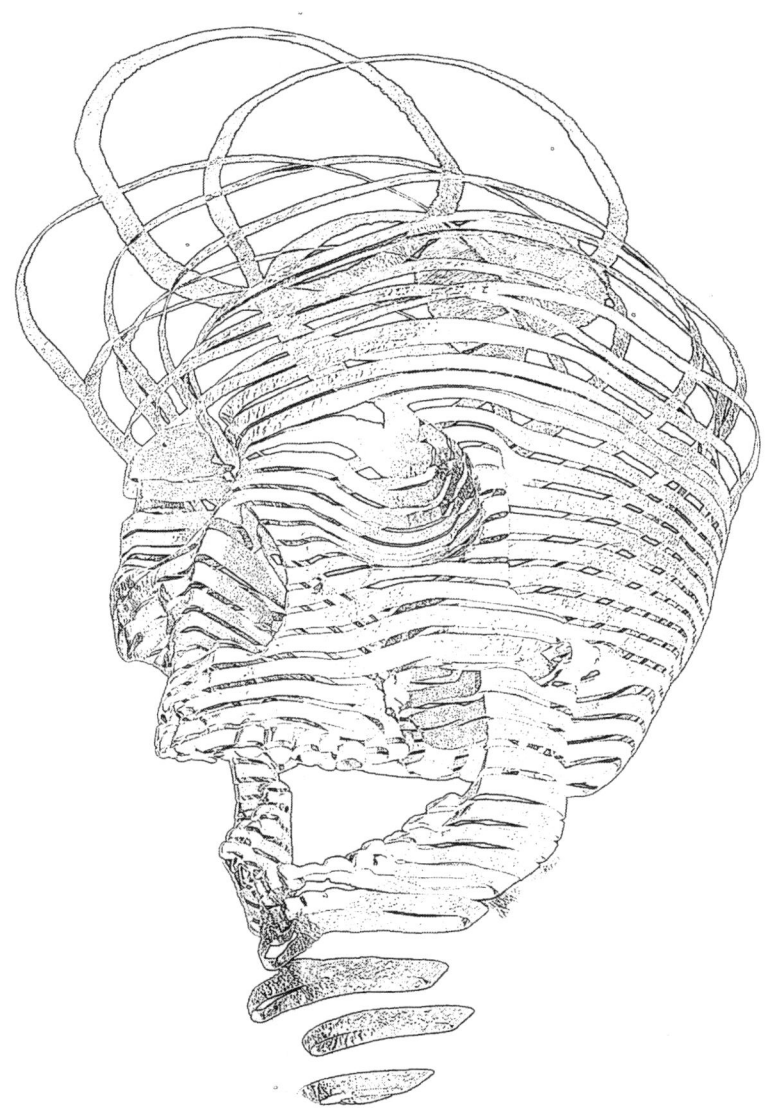

The longer I'm alive, the more I understand death.

Don't be afraid to die; you've done it many times already. Seriously. The observable universe has existed for thirteen billion years - I don't think there's a need to worry. It's all coming and going, breathing, together. Fearing death is fearing birth.

I believe a core aspect of conscious living and spirituality is accepting death. You stop struggling, stumbling, stepping over others to prolong your life. It's a conscious decision to exit the stampede of modern civilisation. And it's not that you no longer feel afraid of dying, rather, deep within, you understand it will happen any moment now, and that's okay. You relax a little, breathe, smirk, knowing there's no outrunning this inevitable conclusion. It brings on a novel perspective in which you realise how unnecessary it is to be so destructive. You mindfully decide the continuation of your existence will no longer be primarily a matter of survival but enjoyment.

I will not allow a depressing world to rob me of the comedy of life.
I will smile even upon my departure, flying through space and time
in the astral plane, laughing all the way home.

The only concern I have regarding death is the possibility of a hangover.

Less than a hundred years from now, you're done; finished. Your possessions, achievements, body - all of it gone. Nothing will remain of your insignificant existence, beside your actions today, which will ripple, however small, for eternity throughout the lives of many.

A global catastrophe like the outbreak of a deadly disease or a natural disaster is nowhere near as destructive as the panic of a species afraid of death.

Death will humble you.

SPIRITJʊÀLITI/

---•·••◆••·•---

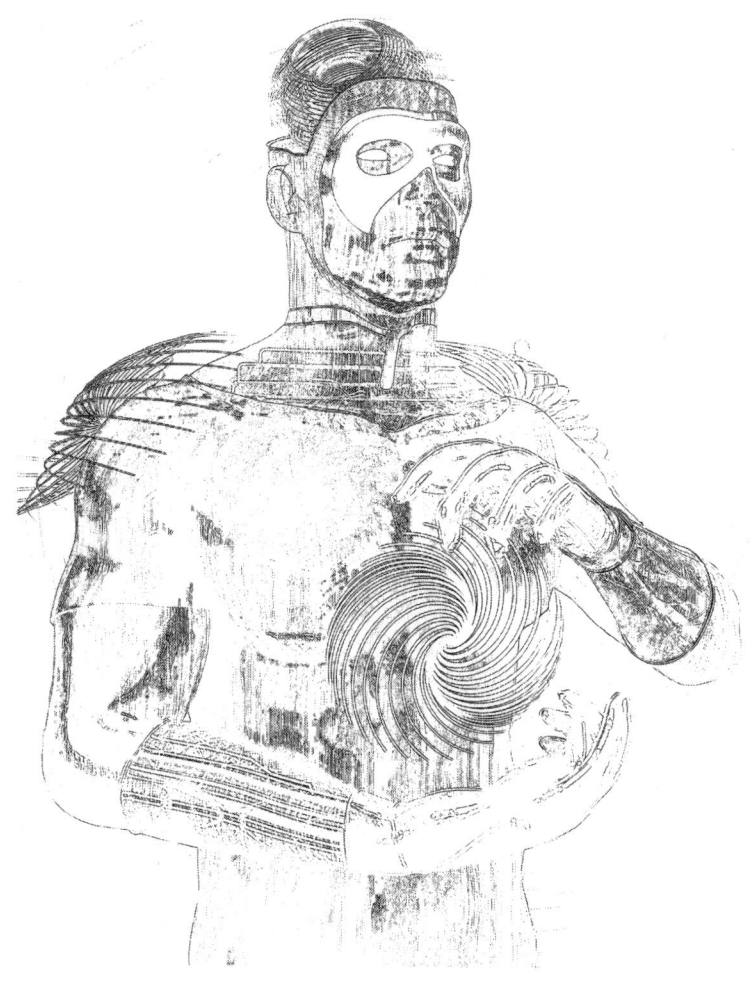

Perceptively, take a step back. Alter your view from ego, which presents a world of words, and look around where you currently reside. Marvellous, isn't it? The inanimate objects, the lively critters, the sound of traffic, the light from electronics, the cobwebs - it's all fundamentally divine. What spirituality means is precisely this, a reconnection with what is, without judgement, thought, or contrast for identity. It's the raw ingestion of existence, a peak under the veil separating oneself from oneself. It isn't nonsense. There is an oversaturated market that exploits spirituality, profiting from terming unfounded knowledge, preying on the psyche of vulnerable people susceptible to buying into what they wish to be true, but it isn't folly. That view stems from a misconception as one cements themselves into a material-based reality offering an idea of normalcy for comfort. However, spirituality is an acknowledgement of the mystery. And by feeling into it, flowing with the wind, rising with the sun, moving with the Earth and sleeping with the moon, we find ourselves more than just material, matter or substance without magic. We embody the spiritual like dreams interpret the individual, like how poetry details love, and that's why spiritual practices directly connect one to everything because we remove the person, the dream, the poet, and become rather than translate. That involves honesty, communication, and courage, for you must consciously step into the dark if you wish to know light.

As a study, all there is to spirituality is remembering. You already understand yourself, which is evident throughout your nature; your body knows what it needs to do to grow. That happening is more you than the voice inside your head, which I believe is no different from the flow comprising my entirety. The same goes for the planets, stars, galaxies and the universe. It's one great cosmic giggle. You may think otherwise if you identify the self as the ego, for as mentioned, it involves a perspective tunnelling consciousness through thoughts, which is to be linguistically confined to a matrix. Inevitably, with such an outlook, a feeling of insignificance, anxiety, and perhaps depression will arise, for the external - superb in its nature - is fundamentally defined as separate, which is an ignorant viewpoint because it completely overlooks what you are. If you doubt this philosophy, try meditation, embracing a space of silence. See what's consciously unearthed when you quiet the mind and reconnect with your surroundings. Afterwards, egoically reflect on the experience; examine what you make of what is meant by spirituality because it's your existence that's in question.

Silence provides more insight into your happening than any scientific study or religious doctrine. You can go on about history, physics, evolution, spirituality, God, yadda yadda, or you can consciously redirect your perception to the source in question rather than dancing around yourself with words.

No one is more spiritual than another. If you have ever visited a guru at a gathering and, in the beginning, noticed them watching, staring intensely, you may have felt inferior or judged as if they were reading your thoughts, unearthing your sins, observing your soul, and knowing how mischievous of a primate you've been. But in actuality, when a guru looks off toward the crowd before their lecture, skimming side to side, visually absorbing their surroundings, they're acknowledging themselves by the many shapes and faces staring back. They see their reflection, rendering their being within the collective. There isn't the slightest notion of authority or difference in ability. It's a meditative practice that we all can do in everyday life to ground ourselves spiritually, especially to overcome ego-related issues that may hyperbolise a situation, negatively worsening matters. Regard a scenario in which someone attempts to dominate your social environment through arrogance. Rather than butting heads, realise this individual is another you, human, of the collective source, though misleading themselves into believing a fallacious identity, putting on an act, most likely due to complex psychological challenges, such as struggling with insecurity. So long as their actions do not impede you, leave them be as you honour your space, for it'll all wash over them come time.

In essence, I feel no more special or spiritual than the moth who passed my window; no more profound or significant than the breeze that followed.

Writing about spirituality is contradictory because it's unspeakable, so any translation is misleading. And involved within spirituality is, of course, the notion of the 'spirit' or soul. In my opinion, the idea we intrinsically are an astral entity with an independent identity seems too influenced by ego and therefore fabricated. It further exposes the psychology of our refusal to accept death by clinging to this illusory character we've familiarised as I. However, I could be wrong. We may indeed have an individual astral self that'll persist after the demise of our materialisation, which somehow tunnels consciousness through ego. But, I doubt this, based on personal experience with meditation, where all thoughts cease, along with 'I,' and basic rationalisation of this notion. So, instead, I use the term spirit as a noun to personify the collective happening. My spirit is your spirit, an ethereal body belonging to all, and the more conscious you are of the soul, the more connected you feel to yourself and, therefore, others. That develops empathy, a means of communicating beyond words as you process the external emotionally through mindful imagery. That goes for all beings. You disrobe the illusion of operating as an independent agent and begin to feel the energy of those around you. Their pain becomes your pain, as does their joy. The more relevant this is, the more in tune you are with your spirit, which doesn't imply being more spiritual. All it means is you're simply paying attention to a fundamental aspect of your being as modern society fixates on egoism.

Practising spirituality means expanding awareness. To do so, you ironically don't do anything. It's inaction rather than action, calming your energy as you ground yourself with your environment. There's no need to align chakras, work light, channel higher powers, study how to ascend levels of consciousness or listen to a podcast of some guru blabber on about something. It's merely sitting where you are now, in your suburban home, half-dressed, listening to police sirens and dogs barking. Take as long as necessary, for your mind will eventually settle. Afterwards, you'll feel revitalised, like you're elevating two inches off the ground with the sun's warmth in your core. But slowly, the ego will creep back in, and, well, you'll be back to making a fuss of things. To practise spirituality is, in a way, to live on multiple levels of perception. Here, you have your common viewpoint, associated with being someone, having beliefs, truths, meaning, significance, rights and wrongs. However, beneath that illusion lies the eyes of the soul, which you open whenever necessary to attain the beatific vision.

Sunday, early morning, incense, music, a clean space, how simple, how blissful.

We ought to encourage self-awareness as a society if we desire to create a more pleasing environment. It's a focus that could help numerous children transition into functional adults and for adults to mentally and emotionally overcome unacknowledged challenges impeding maturity. But for whatever reason, most likely money and control, spirituality is omitted from the education system indoctrinating young minds into a matrix. And the matrix, the 'computer scripts' running within a human, has plenty to do with our mystery as it is the code to our reality.

Inhale. Exhale. You are an embodiment of change, a representation of the flow, and in that disorder, free. Worry is unnecessary, you see? What is now will soon pass, as it just did, and will do so as long there is what is. You are that uncontrollable force, a perpetual happening transitioning through energy. Everything leads to everything, and as a part of everything, you're never alone. We're waves to the same ocean, of the same source, heading the same way. Inhale. Exhale. There's no need to worry.

Learning about oneself takes a great deal of unlearning.

Whether on top of a mountain in the lotus position or stuck in traffic, the moment is ethereal.

One moment of complete presence is a life well-lived.

After awakening, be sure to get out of bed.

Wise teachers know themselves to be students.

/ˈMEɪTRɪKS/

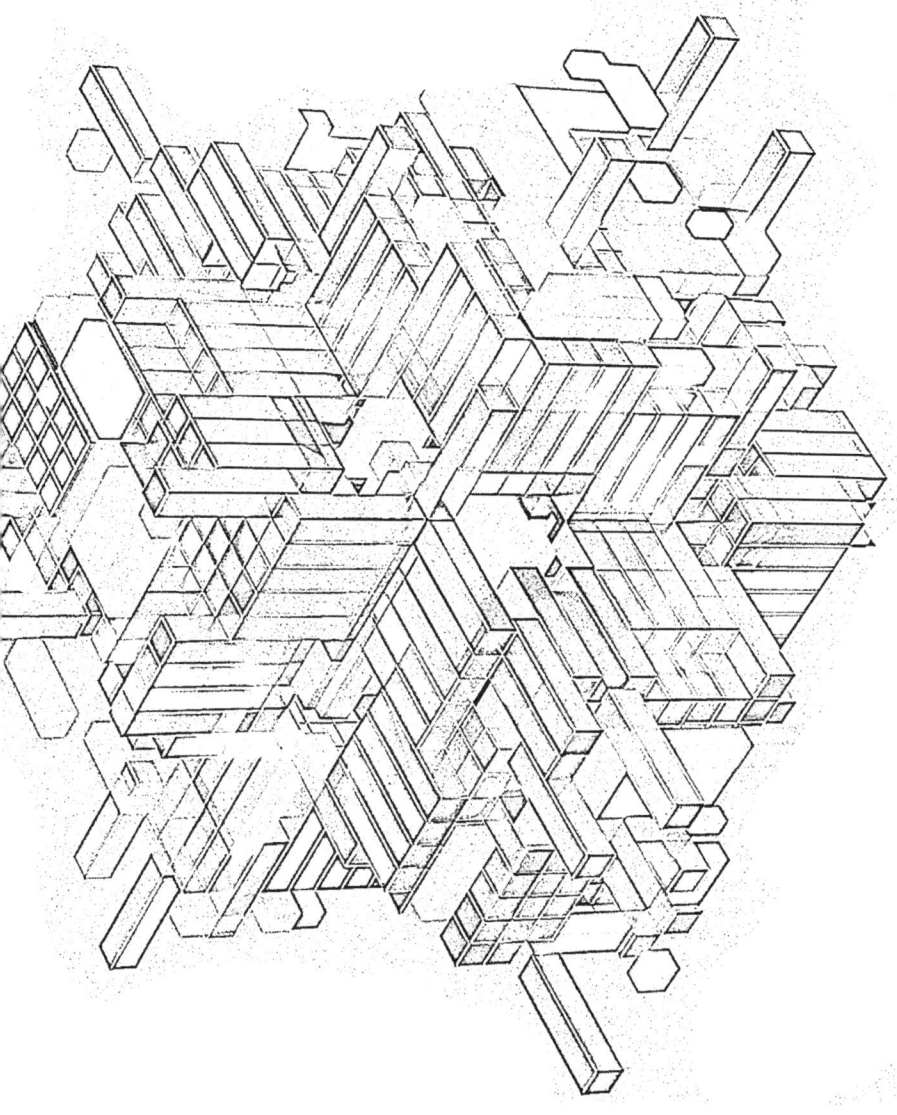

Every human operates from a matrix. We have all been culturally conditioned and linguistically inducted into an ideological system that translates the world before us, perhaps bar those born deaf and blind. It's the process of observing the magic before you, the nature of the physical, yet only seeing 'things.' The same goes for actions, as the activity you perceive isn't a fraction of what's happening. Consider how surreal it is to place your hand on a tree. From an everyday perspective, not only do we limit it merely to the visual display of apparent separate three-dimensional organisms physically interacting, but it is also verbally and symbolically distorted to the terminology of hand and tree, along with the culturally associated meaning. Why this matters depends on your interest in your human experience.

One slight alteration in perception, and the universe transforms.

Without knowing this illusion, you're vulnerable to deception and manipulation. Like a virus to a computer running scripts utilising binary code, a human mind is easily susceptible to equivalent programming. This is noticeable within many trivial aspects of everyday life, along with the extremity of modern civilisation. Consider individual desire, the degree to which someone wants something in particular, such as money, and the basis of economic systems, such as capitalism. Both involve information that, if unconsciously ingested and projected, eventuate into mindless operations, for they'll lack basic human understanding, such as empathy, as information is primarily filtered through the matrix. As a result, people approach one another as democrat, republican, capitalist, socialist, atheist, religious, Black, White and so on, instead of humans or, better yet, anomalous cosmic manifestations originating from the mystery sourcing existence. It eventuates into confusion as we overcomplicate matters and self-understanding without realising.

A haze of beliefs cover the bridge connecting self to other, and from a loss of vision, paranoia develops in the form of egoic chatter, so human interaction lacks vulnerability as we fearfully hide behind a wall of 'truths'.

World peace is theoretically attainable within the hour. All that's required is a change in attitude. Practically, however, it's impossible to convince anyone because we're all too greedy or selfish or stupid or lazy or deluded by some ideology to budge. Nothing is preventing humanity from uniting but humanity. Reflect upon the matter of overconsumption. So many people nowadays have far more than they need, yet the cultivated response of society is to celebrate it as a representation of freedom, honouring capitalism, emphasising the right to go out and earn as much as possible. It's manipulation at its finest, diverting attention away from the gluttonous mentality influenced by acclaiming 'freedom.' Look at a housing crisis; hard-working families become homeless, but wow, isn't it inspiring and wonderful to see those who capitalise on the loss of others living with more than they need? It's a psychological conundrum. The matrix raises generations to recognise and value individual liberty within materialistic intemperance that when overconsumption is in question, people feel it to be an attack on freedom. They scream communism whenever someone accentuates their superficial behaviour because they haven't the strength or awareness to admit their priorities are phoney and shallow. The lifestyle they're addicted to, influenced from a young age by corporations, is about aggrandising oneself financially to indulge more frequently. Multiply that by the billions of people, and you have a suffocating world as everyone tries to squeeze through the same door. And for what? We're all going to perish from this mystifying experience we call existence. But hey, at least some of us drove fast cars, owned a few homes, and kicked our feet up watching television while eating garbage, right? We must get our priorities straight, consciously unearth the underlying meaning of our decisions, desires, and beliefs, or continue selling ourselves to a mindless and soulless system in exchange for supposed momentary pleasure.

The major flaw with all political and economic structures is within the system's culture. If a society's ideas and customs imposing whatever theory neglect hosting an education system encouraging self-understanding through conscious interaction, it mutates into an artificial operation dehumanising the involved. For example, capitalism deforms into destructive consumerism. That is our predicament. Of course, consumption is economically essential, but have you taken a step back to observe what's consumed by the majority and why? Most of it is senseless considering the lack of environmental or health benefits, implying people do not value themselves, or know themselves, so they become consumers. They even become products of the products they consume. It's a matter of confusion, crippling the positives of capitalism. Currently, people are buying 'NFTs.' They're exchanging their time and energy, the only legitimate currency for money, to purchase nothing.

We shouldn't overlook this; it's not something to shrug off by focusing on monetary growth. It's a monumental psychological revelation of how unwell the collective psyche is regarding our consumption, direction, and uncertainty of what we want or who we are as we live through ideology. We are so empty and meaningless that we're now capitalising on seeking fulfilment in both materialistic possessions and conceptual acquisitions for identity. That's a shallow objective, and ideally, if we're interested in our betterment, our novelty and innovations would concern technological advancements and artistic creations that positively enhance the human experience, not revolve around identity or status due to feeling incomplete.

To profit oneself, one must know themselves. Self-interest, therefore, means first to clarify the self, which, in doing so, you realise the intrinsic, symbiotic relationship the self has to the other and its environment. That true selfishness is to act selflessly. Unfortunately, however, what we're seeing out in the world is an absence of self-awareness, which immediately faults capitalism because a misunderstanding of who one is corrupts the cynicism involved with the economic system. Capitalism can't work unless the self profits, but we're not seeing self-profit; we're seeing self-destruction.

Capitalism is a vehicle we're too drunk to drive. There's no direction - we've fogged the windows and interior with ignorance and unresolved psychological problems that we can't see where we're heading or whose hands are on the steering wheel.

Even what we fantasise and imagine rarely transcends the matrix, for most dreams concern the game. We've restricted the most potent, innate human tool and paid the price by living a reality lacking substance. People dream of making a million dollars, which is so trivial to this domain of experience. Yet, that's arguably one of the most sought desires - to accumulate an overwhelming amount of money in a universe of magic. Society is scripted like this, pursuing unexamined desires implanted by culture rather than soulfully sourced. It's the notion of following the herd to remain safe. Go to college, attain a degree, start a career, purchase a house, get married, have children, repeat, recycle. It's human farming for institutions and organisations created to serve civilisation. And it does just that and more, as most decisions and emotional reactions from the average adult are culturally sourced and not internally processed. Look at how people are so easily offended, not because they genuinely feel hurt, but because an external source has told them to find their predicament insulting. Their thoughts are copied and pasted from others, their minds printed by the matrix.

The degree to which the matrix dictates our interpretation of the external goes as far as the universe itself, for when the average mind observes the night sky, they overlook their involvement with translating what's perceived. For the universe isn't *'the universe.'*

We have to stop lying to one another; seriously, stop. We're all human. We know each other's secrets - the anatomy and psychological intricacy - so there's nothing to hide. We may differ slightly in gender, sexuality, and history, but ultimately, we're the same bizarre, beautifully hideous creatures of Earth. So I have zero interest in playing the social game of fabricating a character and story that has me opposing you. It's such a tasteless reality. There's no fun or real engagement involved. It's so phoney, so immature to go around showcasing our egos, masquerading as anything but a human, putting forth a front that separates even ourselves from ourselves that we end up confused and destructive.

This ordeal of ripping each other apart symbolises how much we unconsciously cannot withstand this narrative that's been going on for far too long. We claw at each other because deep within, we want out; we want to liberate the frightened animal raging throughout our minds and return to the wild. We can feel that when we're not drugged by all the trash sold to us - when we're not high on Netflix, social media, processed foods, news, and everything else jammed down our throats. We feel it when we lie under the stars, reminded of how there's more to life than this lie we're living.

I don't believe we fundamentally live in a society, for there are no humans around. Generally speaking, we don't have meaningful connections and conversations. We're disconnected soulfully, malnourished from authentic substances and jacked up on linguistic nonsense. And it's mentally taxing because we're already pressured enough from our unusual predicament of being this conscious in a mystery that debilitating our mental health with an elaborate social hoax is too much; it's too much.

Look, I bleed, cry, feel pain, sorrow, embarrassment, anger, and jealousy. I have no idea where I'm going, where I'm at, how long I'll be here and if I'll make it. So I'm coming on to you not as Travis, not as this structure of words and labels held by some illusory status; I'm meeting you as another human; another vibrational form of energy materialised with the same complexity of ingredients as yourself. And with all my heart, I welcome you as you naturally are.

Living? Who's living? All I see are people seeking the most comfortable place to lay down and die. Mortgage, marriage, career - these are sacrificial rituals of the individual; they're nails to the coffin falsely sold as the modern dream.

The education system creates products for businesses. There's a bunch of frauds marketing themselves as experts for monetary reasons. Go to university, walk the library, drink those lattes and write those essays. But if you have no interest in turning inwards, consciously going where no one's travelled before, into the depths of your mind to unearth raw thoughts on the subject you love, who are you kidding?

Many adults in my society have the emotional maturity of a child.
This is no insult; I mean it as a sincere observation.

I'm tired of money. I'm tired of this system. I'm tired of the politics, celebrities, experts, religions, and gods. I'm tired of this unconscious, dishonest, avoidant, band-aid fixing, instant gratification-seeking mentality dominating the collective psyche. I'm tired of society. I'm tired of capitalising on another's loss. I'm tired of how all news reporters speak the same. I'm tired of the Truman show. I'm tired of the vernacular and syntactical manner of my culture. I'm tired of trends. I'm tired of people acting spiritual. I'm tired of people marketing self-help, monetarily profiting on the vulnerability of others. I'm tired of explaining a perspective to those who do not care to understand. I'm tired of lies. I'm tired of the arrogant, fragile egos exerting dominance. I'm tired of hypocrites refusing to admit the contradictions of their morality. I'm tired of overly sensitive individuals who can't take a joke. I'm tired of reality. I'm tired of words. Blah.

I realised, in my twenties, that a portion of my naivety as an adolescent was not a cause of my youth but a matter of my blind trust in my elders, for the adult world is a complete sham. There's nothing mature about it; hardly a grown person in sight. It's ludicrous and obscene, filled with emotionally undeveloped, ill-disciplined, avaricious, unconscious cultured thinkers. There are many liars, many ignorant minds avoiding self-confrontation, afraid of silent darkness, masquerading as knowers upholding a matrix to keep themselves from being consumed by the unknown dwarfing their existence.

Some sink, some swim, though most stay afloat by drowning others.

There's nothing remarkable or impressive about having more than you need, especially in a world where it'd be wise to consume less.

To the youth, don't be deceived; the adults have no idea what they're doing and have forgotten how to dream.

A child reaches a certain age, and the system immediately indoctrinates them into a reality centred around progression. 'Go here before there, do this, then that,' and this perspective moves like a virus throughout their psyche. It overtakes everything that even romantic love becomes a process of achievement. It teaches them to favour instruction over intuition, discouraging introspection. It ousts their inner artist, hindering creative thought by emphasising the material. It degrades them, modifying their essence as a descendent of the fantastic imagination, full of curiosity and mystery, into a servant of an outdated matrix, roleplaying a character dishonouring their nature.

Degree, career, partner, marriage, mortgage, children, promotion, survive, retire, wait, what? Die.

I'm a horrible employee. I'm too human.

I know people who have replaced their veins with wires. They're reliant on systematic thinking, even referring to science to understand attraction, intimacy, and love. They talk about formulas backed by research and statistics. It's horrifying. I can't imagine how soulless and boring sex must be for them. "I am calculating twenty-two more thrusts before I fulfil my biological duty with this adequate specimen, in which I was chemically encouraged by a sequence of reactions prompting endorphins.." My lord, how trivial and depressing.

This civilisation is full of lazy, weak-minded, ill-disciplined, self-inflicting victims seeking identity through attention and comfort in consumption. Everywhere I look, there are deniers refusing to admit their selfishness, placing blame on anything bar themselves, from terms to ideologies to other people.

/ˈjUNIVəS/

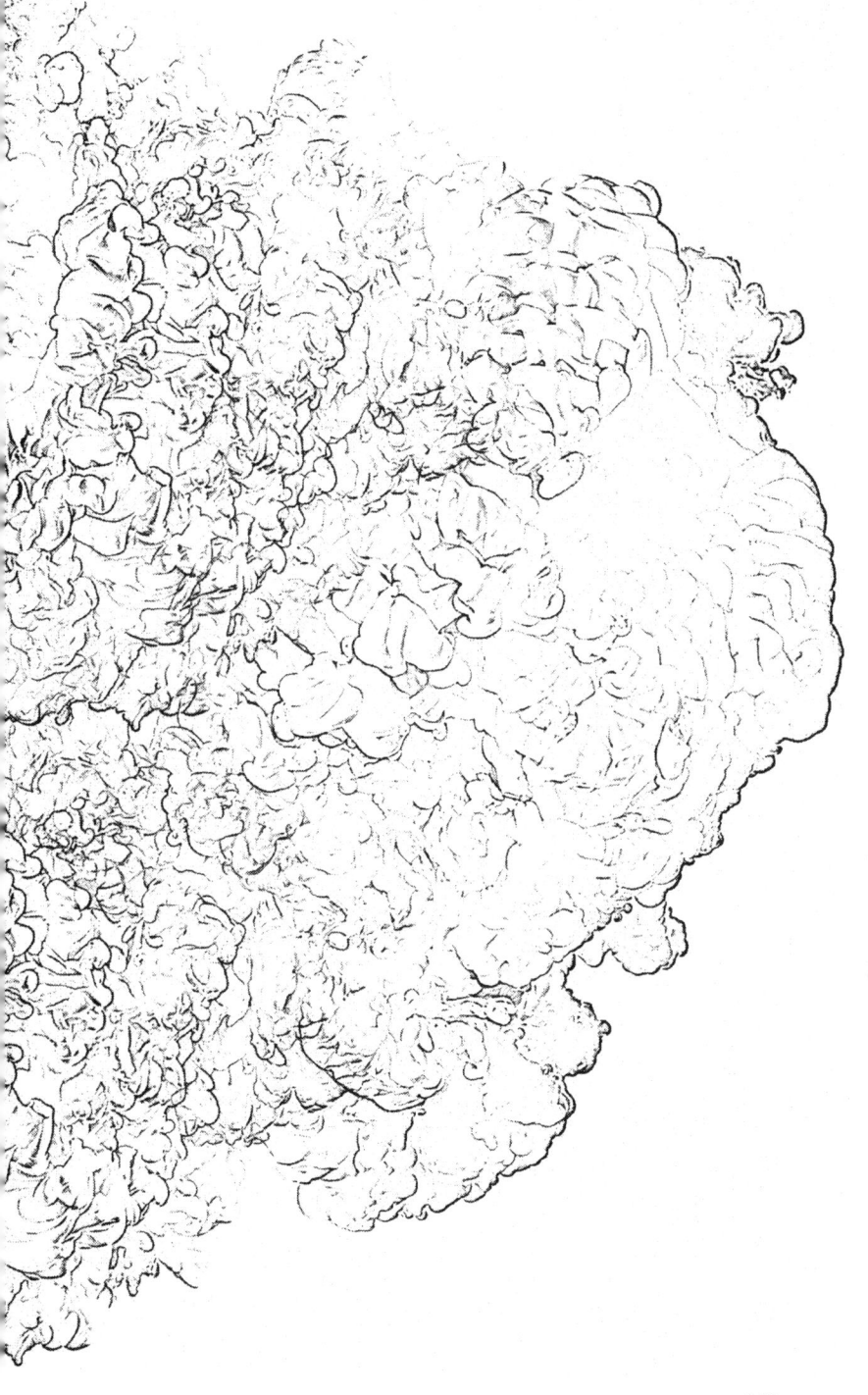

What exactly is the universe? Isn't it just, wow? Astonishing. Fantastical. We can pretend we're not primates blabbering on, hallucinating a reality, and believe it's stars, planets, matter, gravity, space, exploding, expanding, and so forth, but that reveals very little. The *naked universe*, in its raw form, before humans clothed it, is weird. Think about the fact this is happening. There is such thing as such thing. This ineffable field of activity termed cosmos is too unreal for even the imagination. Yet, it exists, whatever that means. Although I can propose philosophical ideas for potential understanding as I have throughout this book, I think it's more insightful to sit in silence and acknowledge its enigmatic nature. To star gaze alone or in good company. That'll present more clarity than the concept of God or any scientific theory like the Big Bang and inflation.

For it is enormous, dwarfing our trivial human world. That's not to prompt discouragement. Be curious but humble. Recognise yourself as a part of a happening greater than whatever matrix you've adopted. I realise that when I observe astronomy-related photos showcasing the universe. They're an exclamation mark to the rhetorical question: "what are we doing?" The division, violence, gluttony - stampede that is modern civilisation, what are we doing!? Look at this place, from the earthworms to the black holes raging in space; wow.

From which we came, we cannot explain, for we are mysterious, so here we stand, dreaming.

Asking why or how may not be the best approach to understanding the universe. Those questions may not even make sense as they are merely human complications. There may not even be an origin. However, commonly assumed by most thinkers is the notion of being able to explain nature, as if our means of rationalising the external is fundamental. Mathematics, for example, is only applicable to organisms attuned to pattern recognition, calculation and measurement. Therefore, it implies the universe to be more about language than mathematics. That's ludicrous to a mathematician, who'd probably be on the edge of their seat, ready to argue such a statement. Although, to overlook our involvement in what we assimilate and define as truth is ignorant. The universe appears the way it does because that's how we see it, and if we want to witness it nude for what it really is, we'd have to die. Otherwise, it'd be like trying to see an eye floater directly. It changes based on our changes. I mean that respectfully too. I am a lover of science, though I realise whatever the experiment, the results, or the truth, it is only that to a human.

I recognise this with the rising popularity of simulation theory. How else would the universe appear to a mind living in an age of computers, artificial intelligence and virtual reality? Of course the universe is simulated to humans surrounded by such ideas, for our thoughts become the universe. In many years, novel thinking influencing innovation will eventuate into a universal model we 21st-century people cannot begin to fathom. In such a future, the universe will be something else. Once a creation, to an accident, back to design remodelling the concept of God through simulation, and soon, novelty. Hence, the connection between the mind and the universe. Both are seemingly inter-related and symbiotically reactive. They transform together. To a degree, that's evident when acknowledging no one perceives the same universe. We are, from this perspective, living in a multi-verse. What is true to you isn't necessarily true to me; the same goes for what is real. That thought is crucial when philosophising the difference in dimensional perception regarding truth. How does the universe appear to an ant, fish, human, bird, or fifth-dimensional creature hailing from another galaxy? How accurate and legitimate are our measurement tools outlining what's possible and factual? To a super-intelligent species, far more advanced than humanity, physics may be so eight-hundred million years ago.

If I came across an interstellar travelling alien who I could somehow perceive and communicate with and were asked by this entity what humanity's most profound understanding of the universe is, I wouldn't answer physics, mathematics or describe God. Instead, I'd tell it a joke and do a little dance. That feels most true, even though it makes no sense from an analytical perspective. But such innate responses reveal something deep behind the veil that other cognitive tools, brilliant as they are, cannot express. It is the 'it,' the flow, known not logically but intuitively, and expressing or embodying just that is to reveal the face of the universe. For it is a grand activity, a cosmic giggle, and we, organic life, are punchlines to the joke. You're either in on it, making light of the dark, nonsense out of sense, or taking everything, along with yourself, so seriously.

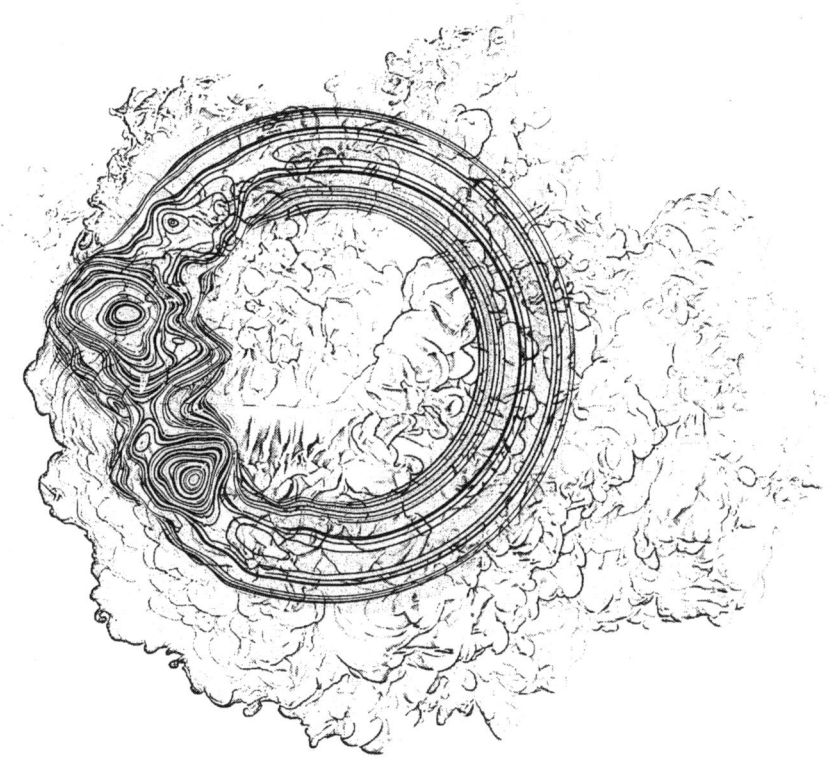

Strictly according to human logic, if infinite universes exists, offering infinite possibility, there's potentially a universe where alternative universes are non-existent, which contradicts this proposition along with our existence.

*How amusing of you to define what's possible. Please, while
you're at it, do explain the universe.*

The world is not absolute. Reality is not fundamental. Science, math, religion, politics, economics, and what have you aren't transcending. The 'universe' you know isn't the naked universe. It is an assumption, a projection from the information registered by your senses and cognition. That is why I, out of emotional immaturity and egoic stupidity, get irritated by half-assed realists cementing logic in the illogical situation that is existence. To rationalise indisputable truth on the foundation of primate assimilation is ironically irrational. There's nothing normal about what's happening. The extreme straight-thinkers reassuring their intelligence by worshipping objective truths are as delusional as the mentally disturbed individuals attempting to lose themselves in fantasy to avoid the transient reality.

I could leave it to the universe, but I feel the universe is leaving it to me, hence me being here.

You wake up as a cosmic anomaly, momentarily physically emerging from vibrational energy, in a chaotic field of activity where stars are dying, black holes are raging, and you start dancing. And it makes sense. I'm unsure why, but it does.

The universe is a matter of consciousness, and for many people, it expands no further than the streets they walk and the idea they have of themselves.

//ĖILIəN//

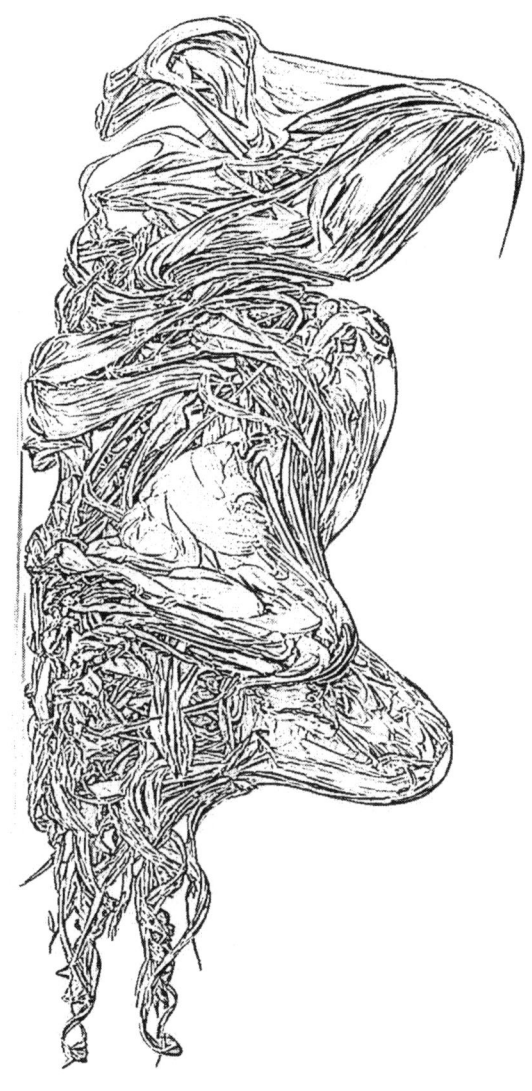

Extraterrestrial life is exciting to imagine. What else exists out there in the vastness of space? How ancient are they? Are they comprised of the same elements as ourselves? Are they even made of matter? Although we currently cannot say for sure, it's unlikely we earthlings are alone. That predicament would be more bizarre than the other. The fact Earth has sprouted all kinds of organisms through nature by the billions suggests life in the universe is not recherché. Sure, we humans are yet to encounter a creature from outer space, though that may have more to do with our inability to sense or realise their presence. After all, what does an interstellar travelling species look or feel like? Especially one that does not arrive by an asteroid as a bacteria-like form but intently via some means of space travel? Perhaps they are to us what we are to the tardigrades living in dewdrops. It is, therefore, naive to automatically assume human interests are relevant when philosophising the characteristics of a non-human space travelling species, as these entities may exceed our imagination. However, understandably, what else do we have but the imagination to consider such beings? To rationalise based on what we understand? Earth is a little secluded paradise in the cosmos; all we know is what's here.

If I were to philosophise such a capable species, I would argue them to be hospitable, not hostile. The idea of space travelling conquerors arriving to impregnate our women and enslave our men seems highly unreasonable. I think the development required to traverse space is impossible to achieve as a divided civilisation, and division indicates a lack of wisdom, connection and empathy. Unless these beings travel space naturally or some other way, the amount of intellectual unity, resources, time and power needed for such an unfathomable task while avoiding extinction or regression is vital. As well as this, the psychological impact - if they have a psyche - of travelling the universe would surely match the spiritual significance of ego-death. To think one would maintain trivial intentions that many humans do in this matrix, such as accumulating wealth or controlling others for superiority while witnessing the spectacles of space, is improbable. The face of the universe up close reveals too clear a reflection to continue believing oneself as fundamentally singular. Therefore, if aliens arrive one day, I'm optimistic they will come in peace.

Regarding arrival, I doubt aliens entering our airspace will be the most probable. If what I suggested is close to their nature or mindset, and they are compassionate, then appearing in our skies is quite intrusive. Imagine waking up, following your usual routine, driving to get a morning coffee, only to see a ufo descending above. Humanity would be a deer in headlights. You probably wouldn't need your morning coffee.

Consequently, their introduction could be a little more thought-out and less sudden. Perhaps they're already awakening us to their presence and have been for thousands of years as they integrate themselves into our reality. Maybe aliens are behind our rapid cognitive evolution, not in the sense of mad scientific experiments, as that would be most unethical, but gently through intoxications, such as psychedelics or language. Because it does appear the cognitive development of our species involved a soft push from behind, considering how far we've come in such a short amount of time. If the theory of evolution is to some degree correct, and we evolved this way, going from swinging trees to filing tax returns and running stock markets within a few hundred-thousand years isn't normal relative to our earthly cousins and predecessors. Something extraordinary happened. And I doubt it's as simple an explanation as saying we Homo sapiens love to travel and happened to encounter suitable conditions for nuclear physicists and artists to eventuate. To our knowledge, that's an extreme consequence that has never before occurred throughout the history of nature. Hence, it isn't too wild to question the involvement of extraterrestrials in our past or today. I'm not saying to believe it, but entertaining the possibility is warranted.

A weird thought to consider regarding aliens is humans. Are we the only ones? Or is there a 'cosmic cookbook' where humans form with the proper planetary preparation, star ingredients, and natural circumstances? If the latter is true, some aliens could be 'us.' That'd be quite the encounter, especially if their civilisation were younger than ours, yet mentally and spiritually far more developed. Imagine meeting another person from another galaxy sharing the same complexity, though they hail from a united civilisation in which suffering is only made known by nature's wrath, not each other. How embarrassing for us. It would make us seem like we have a child's emotional intelligence as we wage wars over power, Gods and control.

Extraterrestrials, at least to my awareness, are unknown for now, though the thought of them is a reminder of our situation. We are in a universe, *of a universe*, and no matter how much we feign oblivion, we are shrouded in mystery.

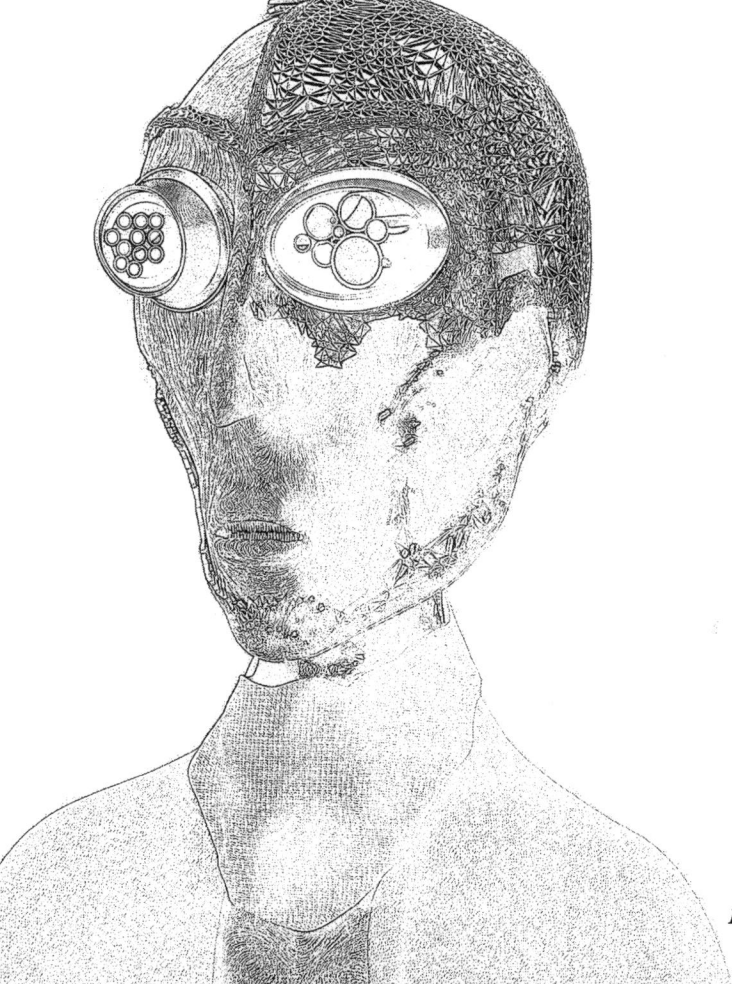

Aliens could be all around us; we just haven't the ability to know whether we're within their presence.

Modern man has made an alien out of himself.

/ˈKɒNʃəSNIS/

I wasn't going to write about consciousness. I don't know where to begin. Thinking or discussing the subject is like looking within to see who's looking. All I can say is that I'm aware. I'm receiving and transmitting. I'm here. And this intensifies the less I think for my state of being returns to, shall I say, wholeness? I'm not bouncing around as an ego, contorting awareness; I am the awareness. But what and where is consciousness? What does it mean to be aware? I obviously have no idea; 'I' don't even exist. Although, I believe there are philosophical thought practices and mindful exercises we can entertain to somewhat grasp the mystery of consciousness. One example is meditation, for meditation is pausing and reflecting, which can give way to a profound understanding through being.

No matter where you are, you can meditate. No need to sit on a mountain, pay someone money, or dress accordingly. It's the most straightforward activity of all practices, yet ironically the most troublesome because almost all humans are addicted to thinking, partially due to fear, as we bother ourselves to either hypothesise a potential future for preparation or avoid self-reflection to prevent surfacing what's within our psyche. Either way, we continuously restrict ourselves by living a lie as ego dominates. Silence, therefore, is uncomfortable, stillness feels strange, nothingness seems foreign, implying we subconsciously reject the foundation of our existence. As a result, we're aliens to ourselves.

If you'd like to meditate, don't try, and don't try not to try. Let your mind run wild and consciously go along with it, like patiently following a stallion. It'll probably venture into the imagination, followed by sourcing memories, comically unfavourable ones, then merging them by playing out possibilities of what could have been and what may happen. Stick it out; keep going. Endure the anxiety, the pain, the humiliation, and insecurity. If you need to stop, that's fine. Rest and return when mentally replenished. After some time, days, weeks or months of meditating, you'll periodically encounter moments of complete presence between thinking. It's not something you'll make sense of immediately, as no one is there to intellectualise the experience at that moment, as you become the experience - the moment. However, in hindsight, you'll internally recognise newfound insight from this consciousness-expanding practice that is too ineffable to express verbally. For whatever words are worth, it's spiritual.

Writing this, I'm not attempting to be wise, poetic, or con you into some belief. I'm not trying to convince or sell you anything. I'm being straightforward, sharing my understanding. I encourage you to apply yourself to your happening meditatively and see what you consciously make of your being. Know yourself through yourself. Because if consciousness is, in essence, what we are, then experimenting with consciousness seems most reasonable regarding self-understanding.

Listening to yourself inhale and exhale is more enlightening than what any divine passage or teacher has to offer. Your breathing is spiritually profound. It's a practice spanning hundreds of millions of years that you do so effortlessly. So consciously focus on your breathing. Let it reveal to you what words cannot.

I've encountered what I would describe as an embodiment of consciousness through meditation. One experience, in particular, occurred while walking. I circled my house, focusing on my feet touching the Earth. After some time - I'm unsure how long - 'I' ceased and felt complete. That's probably the aptest way to put it; a feeling of unity and fulfilment through presence. I felt connected to my surroundings; I became my environment. My usual linguistic point of reference in which consciousness springs disappeared. It collapsed and gave way like a floodgate holding back an infinite ocean. Afterwards, I felt like I was elevating two inches off the ground. This experience altered my philosophical outlook regarding consciousness and, therefore, myself. As mentioned while discussing spirituality, I rationalise the idea of a collective consciousness as more sound than thinking of myself as a fundamentally singular anomaly operating individually, separated from the external. Of course, we can propose a theory that involves a higher self existing outside of this realm, belonging to a collective consciousness, but for argument's sake, let's thoughtfully entertain consciousness by suggesting only one possibility is true. Is there a collective consciousness behind, inside, outside, somewhere sourcing the awareness of all that exists? Meaning every conscious 'thing' fundamentally shares the same consciousness? Or, do we each uniquely possess our own? One that has perhaps experienced numerous incarnations or even been born anew through this life? Both are philosophically plausible.

Imagine an ocean, yourself - a wave. You have momentarily materialised from one great source that experiences all. Fundamentally, your consciousness is my consciousness, as goes for all that is; we're one ocean. However, as waves, we have this viewpoint, an awareness that appears singular. We see the beach from different views, yet inevitably, we discover the perspective to be misleading as we recede to the same body of water upon crashing. That is the concept of collective consciousness. With this in mind, you can philosophise innate understandings, such as life formation, intuition, spiritual insight, love and psychological developments, like empathy, by referencing consciousness as a collective source of information shared by all. It's learning and operating throughout everything, from every atom to every planet. Arguably, a biologist may differ by offering a scientific explanation that details cellular activity carrying information from hosts, but that only prompts further questions as it goes no further than biology. Same with physics regarding atoms. Consciousness, however, is transcending. Intuitively, it's seemingly everywhere though nowhere, unlocatable, undefinable, and immaterial. It's philosophically playful. We can take it further with the collective consciousness theory and rationalise what 'is' came from nothingness, as consciousness isn't of any substance, time, place, or identity. Thus our universe, world, art and realm. Hence, ourselves. And this isn't a matter of creation, a concept of God; it's the contrary. It's suggesting every being is behind this happening, and behind that, 'nothing.'

Explaining the phenomenon of love may be as simple as conscious recognition. If I see you clearly, I see myself, and the emotional response is an immense feeling of familiarity, warmth, and joy.

The other possibility I want to write about is a singular consciousness, one unique to your existence. You can think of this as what is commonly meant by soul or higher self - an intrinsic property, coming into being during your physical formation or prior, from a realm unknown to here. This thought complements the philosophy of solipsism, the idea that only you exist as there's no way to prove the existence of the external to the same degree you know yourself to be real. If consciousness is fundamentally as so, then life is a personal dream. Perhaps this whole universe is yours. That reading this book here, my words, is your doing, as I am but a figment of your imagination sourced for some reason only known to your consciousness. I can assure you that's untrue. I am here as you are, but how can you be sure? Maybe you're trying to fool yourself by making this experience appear more objective by creating a character like myself.

Of course, wild thoughts. But it's warranted. From our realm, our understanding, consciousness is absolute, as in, it's the basis of this experience yet ironically, though appropriately, the most enigmatic. You can engage with various states of consciousness, all presenting an alternative reality. That's noticeable through psychedelics, culture, and language, which is why it's vital to understand it yourself. However, there's no comprehending consciousness without wholly embodying consciousness, but once you do that, say through meditation, you cease to be as you become what is without distinction. Euphoric; enlightenment. A return home to source.

If I cannot feel the magnificence of this moment, sitting alone in my room, as I am, in this space, this realm, this period of history, I'll forever seek more as I subconsciously deem the basis of my existence as insufficient.

Either those who govern this world are genuinely ignorant and stupid, or there is indeed a hostile agenda toward the expansion of consciousness, evident in the system progressing and developing humanity.

/TΛIM/

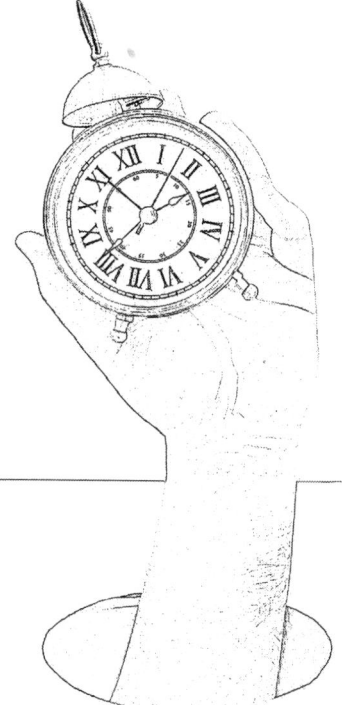

Every word you read, you've changed. You've aged. You're no longer the same as when you began reading this sentence. Nor is the world or reality or truth. Allowing this is what we know as time. It's a bastard. There's either never enough or too much, and then, out of nowhere, it vanishes, along with ourselves. Time mocks us, which can be incredibly mentally taxing, especially regarding the loss of youth. However, I think this stress we feel regarding time is our fault, and by clarifying our understanding, we can create a more favourable relationship with this unknown influence that's indefinitely progressing the space-time-continuum and all within.

To understand time, we must go deeper than the digits on a clock and the calendar. They're merely a system created by humans to help navigate distance and keep records. We must first define what we mean by time. It is, from one perspective, the activity of change made known through observation and memory. If I tell you to go somewhere, and you go, you recognise progression because you can recall the alteration in moments from where you were. Consequently, if you travel that same route repeatedly, factoring in the speed of movement, you can estimate how many moments will occur before you reach the destination. Thus, time. On the other hand, if you're less attentive, often daydreaming, moments will go by unacknowledged. That is why it feels like life flies by during our adult years because we mould into a routine, repeat the day, focus on the weekend, living a few moments a week, unlike our childhood, where everything was new, fascinating - worthy of our attention. We can reference sleep too, where eight hours of unconsciousness can feel like ten minutes, for moments go by unacknowledged. Seemingly, evolution has ingrained this cognitive ability, which is what is known as the biological clock.

From another perspective, a cosmological one, time is a glimpse into gravity. It reveals the mysterious property manipulating space. For example, consider how the pace we're biologically accustomed to here on Earth, as we've evolved from it, involves a certain speed threshold of living or transferring information. Whereas, across the universe, gravitational waves in another solar system may influence a unique velocity, dictating a slower or faster rate at which change occurs. That hypothetically means if you teleported out of this solar system, where gravity works differently, stayed a day, and teleported back, you would be out of sync with the people of Earth, meaning you may have aged a day relative to your biological clock, yet return to Earth a thousand years later than when you left.

As the last perspective, time is the perpetual forward momentum in which we are moving. Like an arrow released in a straight direction, there's a sense we're continuing into a future indefinitely. There is a hereafter that'll soon be now, followed by another. We see it as past, present and future. Yesterday, today and tomorrow, with a dominant focus on the morrow, the arrow lighting up the >yet-to-be-known.> Living by this, we have induced a habit of planning for what's to come through prediction. From forecasting the weather to the next extinction event or end of the world, we're obsessed with looking ahead. As a result, we consciously live in a fabricated future rather than the reality of now.

Regarding these three definitions, we can observe a common theme with time: its dependency on human perception. Although change is inescapable, how we measure and perceive its meaning is entirely on us, implying time doesn't have complete control over our existence.

The only way to waste time is to think you're wasting time.

You're getting older, losing your youth, becoming slower, bearing an appearance less bright. How horrible, right? Time only allows such a short window to enjoy physicality, to move with fresh energy guided by a young spirit, that it's gone before you realise. However, what can we do about it other than accept the flow? To let the stream guide us? Age is natural, and it's a privilege. Be grateful you've been here this long. Enjoy the stages of the body countless others never had the opportunity to undergo. Thank yourself for still being here, growing, learning, and experiencing.

That is to have respect for your losses. Although it's hard to swallow at first, it's a blessing those relationships or spaces which held such emotion, love, joy, and connection ended at the hands of time because of the significant implications that perpetually follow. If nothing ceased, there'd be no beginning, denying the possibility of what you cherished from ever happening. As goes for your life, for what permits your existence, happiness, and loved ones is the possibility of loss - death. So, give in to time, for in return, you're giving into love, novelty and growth. And regardless, who'd want to live forever? It's a vast universe with much to see and many to be.

Thursday, May 5th, what a lie.

As a civilisation, we are obsessed with the concept of progression, ironically without an accurate understanding of what is progressive. It's a culture inducing a belief we aren't where we ought to be, and through changing the environment, usually through destruction, we must, as a species, hurriedly reach some destination or condition, causing society to function with a panic-like mentality. I referenced this earlier as the stampede. Man must advance is the theme. Newer technology, housing, expenditure, growth - everyone rushing about, overlooking one another, living according to a time frame, trying to improve without clarity of how or what needs to improve. We rarely get together; it usually takes a natural disaster. We rarely interact consciously, holding presence to connect. We are just mindlessly trampling, consuming with our eyes set ahead, ignorant of the mess left in our wake. Some argue development in the name of evolution, emphasising survival as if they even know what they mean by that. What are we in danger of, and why must we survive? To what degree is a human inboxed within cyberspace, addicted to electronic screens, disconnected from the environment, more evolved than a member of an ancient tribe wildly dancing around a fire? Because their life expectancy is longer? That's a miscalculation from misunderstanding time. A long life has nothing to do with age but presence. It's a matter of how many moments one is here, now, consciously engaged with existence.

I suggest we collectively slow down, catch our breath and reflect. Let the dust settle. Instead of racing ahead, trying to get to the next stage, and innovating mindlessly, we reconsider what we're doing and what we've done. That way, we can overcome this anxiety, let go of living according to time, and cease harbouring animosity as we compete to succeed. Allow our motives toward growth to be self-sourced; our paths paved intently and honestly. Perhaps we'll see each other more clearly and have a chance to connect. Maybe we'll learn to live again rather than merely exist.

Have you ever thought about the ending of time? Whether the arrow in which we happen will continue progressively 'forward?' There's no guarantee tomorrow will occur, or we won't begin to revert. There's no promise the next ten minutes won't be the last in the known universe. Everything could suddenly stop and vanish, just like how everything perhaps began. It emphasises the mystery of the moment, how the motion of change is unpredictable, which includes you, as an inhabitant of time, this creature spawning from the depths of the unknown.

Until you face your past, it'll remain your future.

/LʌIF/

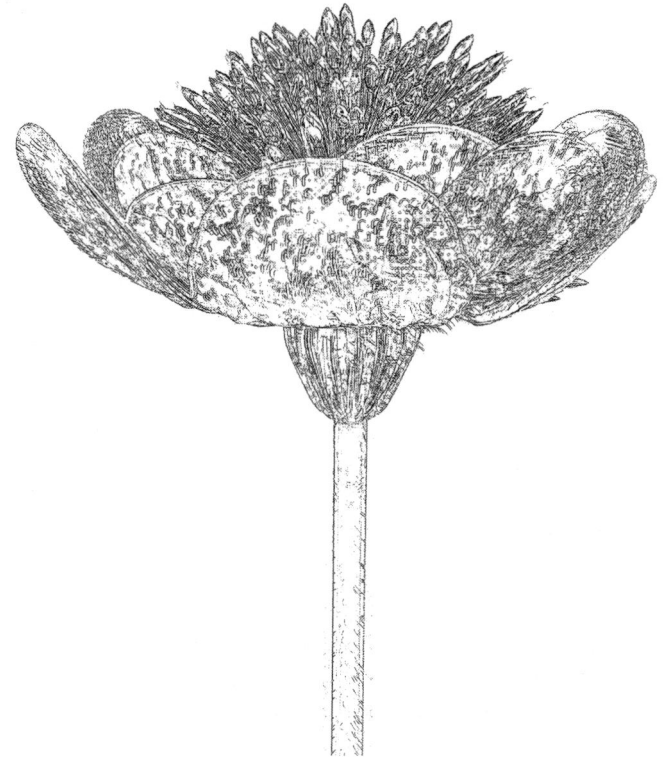

Well, this is it, life. I hope it hasn't been too difficult for you and you're not too overwhelmed by the human game. A lot is going on, internally and externally, which can negatively impact your state of being, especially mentally. It's easy to feel heavy and exhausted, provoking philosophical questions regarding meaning or purpose as you struggle to find the motivation to proceed. After all, from a certain viewpoint, we're all incredibly insignificant. But do consider you're here. Isn't that just..? You know? You're here! There's this, this happening. I understand it's a human perspective, so these questions are probably inapplicable to the naked universe, but looking past non-duality philosophy and wondering how or why there's something rather than nothing is annihilating. My sense of self, understanding, and reality vanish while philosophising such a mindblowing thought. Remarkable. Profound. Also somewhat hilarious. It can be dark, light, great, terrible, animated, dead, nothing or something. But above all, like a child entertained by peekaboo, it's comical, a wild celebration, with the theme being creation. What form can you take? What limits are there to matter? The flora, fauna, fungi, and elements; it's magnificent. And you're a part of it; you are it. Although you may think you're separate, we now know that perception to be fallacious. You are of everything as everything is of you, way back to the 'beginning' of this universe. So I believe a slight smile is most appropriate, right? To respond to the sunshine, moonlight, day and night, loss and love, with a bittersweet smirk because you know, behind it all, you'll be okay, for you're not merely this character, ego, but something extraordinary happening, an ineffable mystery.

We humans have our world, playing this 'civilised' game, chasing never-ending objectives, seeking to be anywhere other than here. It's the life we've created, but it doesn't have to be the life you live. You don't have to follow the order. You can move different, forge a path, and go where your heart feels drawn to explore. Dream your dream. There may be outside noise telling you otherwise, that you're moronic for giving up what they cling to, but they're afraid, for you embody what they've denied, and your presence reminds them of that. That's not to say to live carelessly, but primarily carefree. Live presently, be alive, which means purposefully living your truth. Reveal yourself. How do you want to love? Have sex? Play? Work? Eat? If you haven't the answer, seek further silence in solitude, for this is all ephemeral, ethereal, and rejecting your journey to walk another's as you live according to their wishes would be a metaphysical tragedy.

I entered a different space; turned down a pathless street. I discontinued walking with the mass. My surroundings fell quiet, relationships ended - darkness befriended. Guided by the unknown, I became my teacher, student, and light.

There's not much else to say. It's life; you know it as well as I do - the struggles, suffering, loss, uncertainty, courage, love, joy, amazement. Spectacular chaos. In such an environment, all we can do is let go and try our best. Try to be kind, patient, calm, receptive, and acceptive, but that means acknowledging you'll feel angry, irritated, jealous and even 'evil.' The idea is to comprehend these emotions or feelings by reflecting and examining them so you can find a means to handle their influence. That is to live self-aware, not to deny your humanness, for you are an anomaly physically bubbling from the unknown, hosting an unpredictable psyche. Therefore, self-reflection is wise. Be courageous; show integrity and vulnerability, inspiring authenticity. Journey within, turn yourself inside out, for knowing more about yourself is only possible through honesty. It's not until you put the books down, take the mask off, drop the act, and surrender to the unknown that you can begin to understand your mystery.

You can alleviate a great deal of mental pain by accepting suffering as an intrinsic aspect of life. It's inevitable. You will have your heart broken, feel lonely, fail, be humiliated, and eventually die, but you don't have to suffer over suffering.

People ask me what I want to do with my life as if I'm something separate from life. I am life; I'm alive. I'm living, doing, flowing, moving, growing, changing, dying, happening.

The purpose or meaning of life only comes into question when one isn't living, which indirectly answers the question.

I'm not competing with you; I don't want to have more than you. I don't want fame, money, power or control. I don't care for attention or being remembered. I only want to live simply; to groove, create, flow, support, love and feel loved. Ultimately, I'm just grateful to be here.

I know someone who doesn't do anything deemed productive, yet she's the most sunlit person I've ever met. She often has that look of wonder, like she's visually inhaling everything, even the most 'mundane' things, as she appreciates what is before she isn't.

That's why I say she's the most sunlit person because her demeanour, energy, and facial expressions detail the appearance of someone witnessing their first sunrise. Yet, from the outside, her life is notably unappealing relative to common cultural perception. She once told me she's just glad to be here. That's it. She comes home from her dead-end job, waters her plants, hums away, and plays around. Life to her is floating the ocean waves, making fun of the clouds, and I admire that.

I've paradoxically grounded myself in uncertainty. I've accepted life's chaos and surrendered to disorder for harmony.

I hope my vulnerability inspires your authenticity.

Special thank you to Scott Stephenson and
Jessica Bellantonio.

Hello, my name is Travis, although that's simply an arrangement of lines and a sound I've familiarised myself with that humans make to get my attention. What I mean to say is that I'm something happening here, wherever here is, if anywhere, and very much like you. It may not appear that way. After all, we're separated. Although, underlying that perception, engulfing our entirety is the same source that comprises all. You discover that within love, for love is realising oneself in another. But anyway, look at us here, together - hilarious. It's comical because it's nonsensical. It's a big wow, followed by a booming laugh, perhaps a few tears, then a warming smile. That's life. That's us. And if you're afraid, know it's okay. You can squeeze my hand, for I'm right beside you, embodied within these words, energetically in this realm. It's a wild trip, but I believe wherever we're going, whatever is happening, we'll end up back home, together.

Printed in Great Britain
by Amazon

18500641R00133